THE BED BEFORE YESTERDAY

A comedy

BEN TRAVERS

SAMUEL  FRENCH

LONDON

NEW YORK TORONTO SYDNEY HOLLYWOOD

CHARACTERS

First presented by H. M. Tennent Ltd in association with
Eddie Kulukurdis at the Lyric Theatre, London on
December 9th, 1975, with the following cast of
characters:

Victor Keene	John Moffatt
Alma	Joan Plowright
Mrs Holley	Gabrielle Daye
Aubrey	Frank Grimes
Ella	Helen Mirren
Lolly Tucker	Patsy Rowlands
Felix	Leonard Fenton
Fred Castle	Royce Mills

The Play directed by Lindsay Anderson
Setting by Alan Tagg
The action takes place in Alma's house in Brompton
Mews

ACT I
    Scene 1   4 o'clock on a late spring afternoon
    Scene 2   Four months later; a morning in August
    Scene 3   Tea-time the same day

ACT II
    Scene 1   Shortly after 10 o'clock that night
    Scene 2   About 11.30 the next morning
    Scene 3   10 o'clock at night, three weeks later

Time—1930

ACT I

SCENE 1

Alma's house in Brompton Mews. Four o'clock on a late spring afternoon in 1930

The front door to the street opens into a very small recess between it and the room, with just space for a hat-and-coat-stand with umbrella-stand and doormat. Beside the front door is an oblong window with permanent lace curtains and practical side curtains. Other doors lead to the kitchen and the dining-room. A short staircase leads to a landing on to which open three further doors. The furniture, with some period pieces, and decoration of the room are in keeping with the taste of an owner who is precise and houseproud as well as being very well-to-do. The whole action of the play is during spring and summer, and the chintzes, etc., are in keeping with this. The pieces of furniture essential to the action are a sofa, a writing-table with telephone either on the writing-table itself or on a smaller table close by, complete with the fat, one-volume London Directory of the period. There is also a tea-table in two of the scenes, but this can be folded and placed aside during the rest of the action. This tea-table is in evidence at the opening, with two upright chairs placed on either side in readiness. It is set for two with every-thing ready, including a lidded muffin-dish and a cake-stand. Only the teapot and hot-water jug are missing. (See set plan at end of book.)

Victor Keene is standing up-stage of the table. He is in his late fifties, a gentleman fallen on evil days. He has made his well-worn suit and shoes look as presentable as possible for the occasion. His manner and attitude are self-conscious and rather intimidated; on his best behaviour and anxious to please. Alma enters from the kitchen, carrying a little tray on which are the teapot and hot-water jug. She is forty-five to six. She too has made the best of herself for the occasion, though she is always well-dressed. She is by no means a beauty and very conscious of the fact. She has a most difficult temperament, being liable to fly into uncontrollable fits of anger. At the opening her nervous efforts to face an important, self-imposed situation make her appear possessive and petulant, as she herself explains later on

Alma (*as she comes to the table and deposits the teapot and jug*) There we are. Sit down, Mr Keene.

Victor Oh—thank you.

He waits until she sits, then seats himself. A brief pause. Then Alma gives a little nervous, meaningless laugh

Alma (*with this laugh*) Her-her . . .

Victor (*responding in like fashion*) Her-her . . .

Alma Milk?

Victor Please.

Alma Before or after the tea?

Victor Oh—whichever you—do.

Alma (*decisively*) After. If you put the milk in first you have to guess how much tea. (*Sharply*) Don't you?

Victor Oh, I see, yes. But surely if you put the tea in first you have to guess how much milk?

Alma No, no. Tea first lets you judge the right blend from the colour you get from the milk.

Victor (*giving way*) Ah. Yes. I—see your point.

Alma Sugar?

Victor Please.

Alma One lump or two?

Victor Oh, whichever—one will do, thank you.

Alma I never think one is enough to sweeten the tea.

Victor Oh, very well; if you take two——

Alma I don't take any. Well? One or two?

Victor Two, please. I mean one. One. Thank you.

She hands him his cup

Thank you.

Alma (*pouring her own cup*) It's very kind of you to come and have tea with me.

Victor It's very kind of you to ask me.

Alma I got your address from your sister.

Victor Yes. She wrote to me too.

Alma (*sharply again*) About me? What did she say about me?

Victor Oh, just—she thought I'd like to keep up the acquaintance sort of thing.

Alma (*lifting the muffin-dish lid and offering*) Have one of these. Do you call them scones or scons?

Victor (*guardedly*) Which do you?

Alma Scons.

Victor (*as he takes one*) Yes, I knew it was one or the other. Thank you.

Alma (*starting the genuine conversation*) Mr Keene . . . ?

Victor Yes?

Alma When you came to that hotel at Southbourne a fortnight ago . . . ?

Victor Yes?

Alma Why did you come?

Victor (*obviously*) Why? To visit my sister. Just for a few days. She thought the change might do me good.

Alma When she invited you, did she say anything about *my* staying there?

Victor (*surprised*) No. Why should she? I mean—I'd never even heard of you.

Alma Because she went out of her way to tell me about *you*. Before you arrived, that is.

Victor About me? What about me?

Alma About—well—your past history.

Victor Past history? I haven't got one. (*A little chuckle and he takes a bite of his scone*) Why, what did she tell you?

Alma That you were a widower and—not doing anything and . . . (*She pauses*)

Victor (*with a little frown*) And what?

Alma Well—living on a very modest income, she said.

Victor (*resentfully*) That's true enough. But why should my sister want to tell you that?

Alma (*with nervous irritation*) Do please eat your scon over your plate, do you mind.

Victor Oh. (*Taking the plate*) Sorry.

Alma Scons make the worst kind of crumbs because they have butter in them.

Victor (*examining his scone innocently*) Oh, have they?

Alma I remember when I first saw you in the hotel. You and your sister were having tea with my step-mother in what they call the sun-lounge.

Victor Yes. You came in from giving your little dog a run on the leash.

Alma My step-mother's little dog.

Victor (*resignedly*) Step-mother's little dog.

Alma Personally I dislike little dogs.

Victor So do I. Oh, your step-mother's is quite a nice little dog . . .

Alma It's a horrible little dog.

Victor Oh, is it? I didn't get to know it at all well. (*Amiably*) But if you dislike it why take it for a run on the leash?

Alma Because my step-mother was having one of her bad feet days. (*With nervous irritation*) Besides, it wasn't a run on the leash. How can anybody give a dog a run on the leash?

Victor Oh, a little dog like that, surely? It could run even on the leash. Sort of patter, patter, patter.

Alma You stood up to say how-do-you-do still holding your teacup in your right hand.

Victor (*innocently*) Did I? I suppose I was taken aback or something.

Alma You got in a terrible muddle putting the teacup down and slopping it and having to wipe your hand before you shook with it.

Victor (*fighthing resentment*) I don't know why you should remember that.

Alma It gave me time to take a good look at you.

Victor (*jokingly*) Did you want to?

Alma Yes, I was interested after what your sister had told me.

Victor Why, what more had she told you?

Alma About your first marriage.

Victor My first? I've only had one.

Alma Then it was your first, wasn't it? She said your wife died about ten years ago.

Victor Yes, in nineteen-twenty. Soon after I got back from the war.

Alma I know. Your sister told me all about her.

Victor (*genuinely annoyed*) She had no right to.

Alma You needn't think I asked her. She just told me.

Victor Told you what?

Alma That your wife ruined you by her extravagance. And that's why you're so badly off now.

Victor I'll have something to say to my sister.

Alma Well, it's true, isn't it?

Victor Whether it's true or not. . . .

Alma Don't be snappish with me, Mr Keene. I'm only sympathizing.

Victor (*relenting somewhat*) Oh. Then it's very kind of you and all that; but I really don't see . . .

Alma That it's my concern?

Victor No. Yes.

Alma Don't you want it to be? (*A moment's pause*) I sympathize because I had much the same experience myself. In a sort of way.

Victor Really? But nobody ruined *you*, surely?

Alma Not in that way. (*Pause*) Aren't you going to drink your tea?

Victor Oh. Yes. It's still quite hot. (*He drinks for the first time*) I prefer it cool.

Alma You must find life very depressing. Because you were so well off at one time, weren't you?

Victor (*with a sudden change to candour*) Well, since you know so much about me, Mrs Millet, yes, I was. I had quite a good private income but—it all went.

Alma Your wife gambled, didn't she?

Victor This is my sister again, I suppose? Well, yes, it's true enough. My wife was a born gambler. It was just part of her nature.

Alma (*sincerely and bitterly*) Yes, I know what a curse one's nature can be.

Victor *You* do?

Alma Never mind about me yet. What happened about your wife?

Victor Well, there she was—at it the whole time. Stock Exchange—horses —she used to take trips to Monte Carlo. It was her whole life. She was Australian, you see.

Alma Oh, how sad.

Victor By the time I came back from the war I was pretty well ruined. I'd never done any sort of a job and I felt too old to start.

Alma (*pleased*) Yes. How old *are* you? Never mind, I can guess.

Victor I don't mind your knowing. I'm getting on for sixty.

Alma Oh, is that all?

He does not know quite how to take this. There is a brief pause

More tea?

Victor No, thank you.

Alma There's some cake if you . . .

Victor No, thank you. I don't as a rule have any tea at all.

Alma Poor Mr Keene. (*Rising*) Well, let's sit over here. (*She moves to the sofa*)

Victor (*rising*) I'm afraid I mustn't stay too long.

Alma (*with sudden vehemence*) You've only just finished your tea—not that you've had any. Of course, if you *want* to go . . .

Victor (*anxiously*) No, no—if you really wish to talk to me . . .

Alma (*as before*) What do you think I asked you here for? (*Checking herself*) No, I'm sorry. I mustn't be like that. I promised myself I wouldn't.

Victor (*appeasingly*) Like what?

Alma Like I am. Like I've been ever since you came. Nervous and edgy and abrupt. I did so want to be pleasant. It's sort of over-anxiety. Do forgive me.

Victor That's all right, Mrs Millet. It's best to be oneself.

Alma Not in my case. (*She sits on the sofa*) Do sit down.

Victor sits in the armchair. Alma goes on evenly but always with impatience just below the surface

Yes, I do want to talk to you. About myself. I've led an unusual sort of life. I had a very peculiar childhood to begin with. I was born a Bull.

He looks blankly puzzled. She notices this and takes him up, impatiently

One of the Bull family. Bull's potted meat.

Victor (*to himself*) Good Lord.

Alma My mother died when I was born. They did that half the time in those days. My father wanted a son. He detested me for being a girl. Besides, I was hideously ugly. I always have been.

Victor Oh, come come . . .

Alma Please don't interrupt me all the time. Oh, there I go again. I'm sorry. But that was your fault.

Victor makes a reassuring gesture

I never saw much of my father. He married again. That old Southbourne hotel one. Poor thing, she's got very old and silly. I try to be nice to her; not that I'm nice to anybody for long. Then my father died too. I was brought up by an aunt. Very strictly. I was sent to a convent school. They wanted me to become a nun. (*Angrily and scornfully*) I soon saw to that. Insidious gammon. They were after my money, of course. (*With challenge*) You're not a Roman Catholic, I hope?

Victor Me? No. I'm just a common-or-garden C. of E. sort of thing.

Alma My father left most of his fortune to my step-mother—in trust for me, that is. At the time I only got a hundred thousand pounds.

Victor (*involuntarily*) Gosh!

Alma (*sharply*) What?

Victor Nothing—I wasn't interrupting.

Alma I was a very innocent young woman. I never thought of getting married.

Victor Why not? I'd have thought—(*checking himself*)—no. Please, go on.

Alma Then, when I was nineteen, a young man came along—an absolute scoundrel. Oh, of a very good family—heir to a title, and so on. And I married him. But he was as bad as the nuns—he only wanted my money. Oh, I had a shocking experience. Thank goodness it didn't last long. He very soon got drunk and fell out of an aeroplane.

Victor What a happy release. I hope he didn't spend too much of your money before he—fell out.

Alma He didn't have long enough. (*With a shrewd look at Victor*) So that's still all right, Mr Keene.

Victor So what did you do then?

Alma What could I do? A widow of twenty. My aunt was dead by then, thank goodness. I wasn't going to live with my step-mother. A little of her went a very long way; it still does. So I decided to try again—with George Millett. He was my official guardian. He was twenty-five years older than I was.

Victor Twenty-five? No?

Alma (*in a minor flare-up*) What do you mean "no"? When I say twenty-five I mean twenty-five.

Victor (*hastily*) Yes, yes; I only meant fancy.

Alma (*calming down*) We lived at Reigate for twenty-odd years. He died six months ago.

Victor Oh, I'm sorry.

Alma No, you're not; why should you be? I'm the only person entitled to be sorry and I'm not either.

Victor (*stung into retaliation*) Was *he*?

Alma (*unconscious of any sarcasm*) No; I think he was glad to die. He'd got old and crotchety and he had bad feet.

Victor Oh, these bad feet.

Alma (*sharply*) Why? Don't tell me *you* have bad feet?

Victor No; I meant your step-mother.

Alma Oh, hers are just bunions. George Millett's feet had got past belief. It was all this ridiculous golf. Do you play golf?

Victor Good heavens, no. I can't afford anything like that.

Alma So then I sold the Reigate house and came to live here in London, in this mews.

Victor That's a bit of a come-down, isn't it? Oh, it's very nice and all that. But you say you've still got—well, ample means . . .

Alma You seem very concerned about that, Mr Keene.

Victor I? No. I only meant—is this house big enough for you?

Alma Quite big enough, thank you. It's got two bedrooms.

Victor So I should hope. You surely must have a spare room for a friend.

Alma I have no friends. (*Rising*) I'm a friendless woman. Or, rather, unfriendly. Aren't I?

Victor rises

Victor (*guardedly murmuring*) You're being very friendly to me.

Alma I've got this dreadful sort of nature—hostile to people—almost, oh, I don't know—rancorous. I've had it ever since I grew up, since my first marriage anyhow. I'm embittered. I look for opposition everywhere; I anticipate it. You needn't think I want to be like it. I struggle against it sometimes. But it's difficult to fight against what's—(*she thumps her chest*)—there, inside you; part of you.

Victor (*after a thoughtful pause*) But your husband . . .? I mean, while he was alive—did he—come in for it?

Alma He learnt to turn his back and ignore it.

Victor D'you know what I'd have done. I'd have known you didn't really mean it and tried to make *you* see that too. Sort of laughed it off.

Alma (*thoughtfully*) No-one has ever done that.

Victor Then it's time they did.

Alma But I get like it with shopkeepers and servants. People like that can't laugh at me. All the same, I think you've been very clever.

Victor (*with a chuckle*) First time I've ever been accused of that.

Alma I'll try laughing at myself instead of hating myself. Poor Mr Keene, I'm sorry to inflict myself on you like this. I know the impression I've made on you and oh, I wanted so much not to. You think I'm an absolute shrew, don't you?

Victor Indeed I don't.

Alma (*angrily*) Oh, don't lie to me.

Victor (*reprovingly*) Now, now . . .

He gives a little laugh. Alma doesn't join in the laugh but pulls herself together and speaks quietly

Alma You *must* think I'm a shrew.

Victor No. Well—perhaps I may have, a tiny bit, to begin with. But against that, I think you've got . . . (*He pauses*)

Alma (*rather challenging*) Got what?

Victor (*very tentatively*) Well, charm . . . (*Hastily*) In a funny sort of way, of course.

Alma (*greatly softening*) You really mean that?

Victor I do. I daresay it's hard to believe.

Alma (*sharply again*) Why is it?

Victor No, I shouldn't have said that.

Alma Shouldn't have said I had charm?

Victor No; shouldn't have said it's hard to believe.

Alma Why not, if you really think so. (*A moment's pause*) Well? Shall I go on?

Victor Oh, please do.

Alma (*gentle again and appealing*) Well, what do you suppose I get like, here alone and like I am? I'm lonely. Wretchedly lonely.

Even this rather stupid Victor is wise now to what's up. He decides to play it cautiously

Victor No-one to visit you? No relations?

Alma My only relation is some sort of distant cousin named Lolly Tucker. She's divorced and lives at Ealing and takes lodgers. I'm afraid she's not quite our class.

Victor Oh. Well, what about a companion?

Alma (*suddenly fierce again*) *Companion?* You mean a female one? Some vicar's daughter with chronic adenoids?

Victor (*meekly*) Couldn't you find one without?

Alma No. They all have them. (*Sitting in the armchair*) In any case, another woman? No, thank you. (*Getting down to it forcibly*) I want two things, Mr Keene. I want someone to help me overcome this accursed disposition and I want company; agreeable company. A man.

Victor (*sitting on the sofa*) What—sort of man?

Alma Don't pretend you don't understand.

Victor Mrs Millett, what is this leading up to?

Alma And don't pretend either that you didn't come here today hoping that this might happen.

Victor (*in protest*) Oh, Mrs Millett . . .

Alma Because of my money.

Victor Oh, but I had no idea that you were so prosperous.

Alma Your sister knew.

Victor (*more boldly, in self-defence*) She didn't. She gathered that you were well-off but neither of us had an inkling that you were Bull's potted meat.

Alma Oh, I know that my money is the only possible attraction . . .

Victor No, but . . .

Alma What do you mean "no"? Of course it is.

Victor (*appealingly*) Oh, please—you don't want me to pretend I've fallen in love with you?

Alma No. Any more than I have with you. It's simply that you happen to be the right sort of man. A gentleman. And of the right age.

Victor But, Mrs Millett . . .

Alma Alma, my name is. Yours is Victor, isn't it? Very appropriate too.

Victor No, but hold on . . .

Alma (*incredulously*) Hold on?

Victor No, but please listen. (*He rises*) Here I am, living on a piffling little annuity—two hundred and thirty a year—in a miserable basement flat off the Earl's Court Road. No decent clothes, no decent food. Hardly enough for tobacco. None of the old pleasures of life—no clubs, except my membership of the M.C.C.; I've always stuck to that. Then suddenly this incredible thing happens. *You* come along. I'm given my choice between carrying on the way I am—and you.

Alma You needn't make it sound like a choice of evils.

Victor No—I expressed myself badly. I only mean—ought one to get married just for money and nothing else; well, nearly nothing. Would it be ethical?

Alma What does that matter?

Victor Oh, so long as you don't think it does. (*He sits on the sofa*)

Alma I want your company; you want a share of my money. What has being ethical got to do with it?

Victor Well, if you put it like that how can I refuse?

Alma (*rising*) Then don't refuse. (*Softening greatly*) Oh, please—please, Victor. (*She sits by him on the sofa*)

Victor After all, I don't suppose it would be so—I mean it might turn our wonderfully. I did mean that about your having charm.

Alma (*eagerly, and growing quite emotional*) I can stop myself being like I am; morose and lonely and—blank. I can be happy; we both can. I can get rid of my flying-up and be pleasant and gentle. I'll try so hard to be.

Victor Perhaps I may be able to help about that.

Alma Oh, you will; I know you will. The money won't be the first thing with you for long.

Victor No, it's beginning not to be already. I'm sorry I said I wanted you only for the money.

Alma At least it showed you're honest.

Victor But the way I put it—I made it sound as if you were revolting.

Alma (*almost coyly*) And I'm not?

Victor Good heavens, no; of course not. Not really.

Alma You make me feel happy already. Kiss me, Victor.

Victor What? Oh, yes. I forgot that.

He kisses her formally and briefly on the cheek. She becomes gay and enthusiastic

Alma (*rising*) We can get married at once. In a registry office. I'm not going to be garped at coming out of a church. We won't need a honeymoon. We can come straight back here and settle down. Oh, Victor—how soon can you be ready?

Victor I can give up my flat anytime. (*Rising*) Oh. (*The "oh" is because he suddenly realizes that there is a snag which he has entirely overlooked*) Oh, Lord. There's something else. Oh, confound it—I got so carried away.

Alma (*shocked, challengingly*) Why, what do you mean?

Victor There's someone I'd forgotten about.

Alma Another woman?

Victor No, no. Aubrey. Oh, gosh.

Alma Aubrey? Who is Aubrey?

Victor My son.

Alma Oh, you have a son.

Victor Yes, I'm afraid so. He's dependent on me.

Alma Why? He can't still be an infant.

Victor No, he's quite grown-up—twenty-two, in fact. But he's never—how can I put it?—He's never quite developed.

Alma A midget.

Victor No, I mean developed mentally.

Alma (*less aggressively*) Oh, dear—an imbecile.

Victor Yes. (*Hastily correcting himself*) No, no. No. You couldn't put him away or anything like that. He's just—silly.

Alma You mean he can't feed himself or——

Victor (*cutting in*) —Oh, yes; he's quite active. In fact he's often a great nusiance.

Alma Does he work?

Victor He has worked. In little odd jobs. But never for long.

Alma Well, he can find somewhere to live and look after himself, I take it?

Victor He'll have to, won't he? (*Tentatively*) I mean, he can't very well come along here too.

Alma (*threatening to flare up*) What?

Victor No, I'm saying he can't. But you see, I'm his father. I feel responsible for him. Besides, I'm very fond of him in a way. Don't worry; I'll do something about him. We can't let anything interfere with our—future.

Alma (*very decisively*) Nothing's going to interfere with mine so it needn't think so.

Victor Quite, quite.

Alma pulls herself together with an effort and becomes amiable and practical

Alma Very well then—do you want to be shown your new home?

Victor Oh, please, yes.

Alma (*pointing*) Through there is the kitchen and back door.

Victor Oh, yes?

Alma (*going up and opening the dining-room door*) And this—this is my dining-room.

Victor (*glancing into the room*) Oh, that's very nice and compact.

Alma points upwards at the door nearest up-stage

Alma That front room up there—that will be your bedroom.

Victor Oh, that's very nice, I'm sure. You mean—all to myself?

Alma (*ignoring this; indicating the middle door*) In the middle there, that's the bathroom. (*Pointing to the third door*) And that's *my* bedroom. There's no point in my showing you that.

Victor (*with one of his little chuckles*) Her-her. Not yet, anyhow.

A pause. Alma turns and looks at him, deliberating. He notices this and his jocular manner leaves him immediately. After taking thought Alma speaks as if to herself

Alma I'd better tell you now and get it over and done with.

Victor Oh, please don't say anything you don't want to.

Alma (*half flaring*) I *never* say what I don't want to.

Victor (*appeasingly*) No, no. I think I can guess what you have in mind.

Alma (*still angrily*) What, then?

Victor Well, the—shall I say—the bedroom side of it?

Alma Well?

Victor hesitates

Alma What *do* I have in mind?

Victor All I mean is—a woman like yourself—a widow and still fairly young—that is, compared with women who are a bit older and past it . . .

Alma (*impatiently*) What are you trying to say?

Victor Simply that no doubt one of your reasons for wanting to get married again is that you may still be feeling—how can I put it nicely?—feeling the need of a husband not only in the day time.

Alma reacts with a little shudder. He compromises quickly

Occasionally, anyhow.

Alma And is that what is in your mind, too? As well as the money?

Victor No, no. With me it's entirely the money. I mean it was to begin with.

Alma (*softening again*) Come and sit here.

She sits on the sofa and pats the seat beside her. Victor obeys

I told you about my first marriage, when I was nineteen. I went into it without the slightest knowledge of what happened to a girl on her wedding night.

Victor Oh, I say. You mean nobody had told you?

Alma They didn't tell brides in those days. They observed the Victorian tradition that it wasn't a respectable thing to talk about. Girls had to find out for themselves. (*Bitterly*) I found out. My husband had no consideration or compassion or restraint.

Victor The rotter.

Alma I was forced down and outraged and terribly hurt. Oh I resisted, of course. I had a will of my own already. I scratched his face so badly that he couldn't show it in public for the rest of the honeymoon. But that wasn't for long. He went away almost at once.

Victor (*guardedly*) Well, don't be afraid that *I'd* try to do anything—unpopular—no, what's the word?—discourteous.

Alma (*greatly relieved*) I'm so glad you feel like that, Victor. That was my one and only experience of it; but that was enough.

Victor (*also relieved, perking up*) Oh, well; if that's how you feel, that suits me. But how about your husband—I mean the other, golfing one—Millett?

Alma He was quite willing not to from the first. With me, anyhow. I know he consoled himself here and there. I didn't mind.

Victor There'll be nothing like that with me. I don't want to have anything more to do with a woman even if she isn't you.

Alma You only say that to please me.

Victor No, I don't.

Alma Because, judging by George, quite elderly men still hanker for it.

Victor Not in my case.

Alma (*hardening suddenly and rising*) Because I'm so undesirable?

Victor rises

Victor No, no. That isn't the reason at all. It's simply I've—shot my bolt.

Alma You needn't be sordid. I can't think how any man could ever want to go through that disgusting rigmarole but apparently they do.

Victor (*meekly*) It's his nature. Besides, the world has got to be populated.

Alma (*defiantly*) Why?

Victor Oh, please; there's nothing to argue about. We're in perfect agreement. You don't want to sleep with me; I don't want to sleep with you.

Alma Only because I'm like I am.

Victor You said that before. It isn't true.

Alma (*flying up*) If you're going to contradict me the whole time we'd better not start at all.

Victor (*boldly*) Oh, yes we had. I'm not going to give you up in a hurry.

Alma That's for me to say, not you.

Victor (*holding up a warning forefinger*) Now, Olga . . .

Alma (*in a horrified tone*) Olga?

Victor I mean . . .

Alma Al-ma.

Victor Alma, yes, of course. Now, Alma . . .

He wags the forefinger at her and laughs a false laugh. After a moment she relapses completely and laughs too. She takes him by the shoulders

Alma Oh, Victor—I *knew* you were the one I was looking for. (*She releases him and turns towards the staircase*) Come along: I'll take you and show you your own little bedroom.

Victor Oh, *rather*; yes—thank you.

Alma leads the way upstairs. Victor follows her, his hands decorously clasped behind his back, as—

the CURTAIN *falls*

SCENE 2

The same. Four months later; a morning in August

The room is just as it was before. When the Curtain rises, Mrs Holley, a daily woman of about fifty, is using a carpet-sweeper and singing as she works. After a moment the doorbell rings, she goes and opens it

Aubrey is at the door. He wears an old suit and no hat. His manner is furtive. Aubrey's silliness takes the form of being offensive with the pleasantest of natures and accepting reproach with a fatuous grin. He enjoys using expressions and words which were in those days considered obscene. Beneath his slovenly appearance he is well-bred and not altogether an unsympathetic character

Aubrey (*secretively*) Is she out?

Mrs Holley (*who dislikes Aubrey*) Do you mean Mrs Keene?

Aubrey Yes, of course. Is she?

Mrs Holley She's gone shopping.

Aubrey (*advancing confidently*) Oh, good egg. What about the old man?
Mrs Holley I beg your pardon?
Aubrey My father. I suppose he's had to go, too. To carry the parcels, poor old sod.
Mrs Holley You'll kindly not use words of that sort to me. If you wish to see Mr Keene he's in his bedroom.
Aubrey What, isn't he up yet?
Mrs Holley Of course he's up. (*Dusting the desk*) Long ago. It's jest he likes to sit up there of a morning and smoke his pipe.
Aubrey (*laughing*) I get it. Not allowed to smoke it down here. (*He sits in the armchair*)
Mrs Holley (*aloof*) That don't concern me and it's not for me to say even if it do.

Victor comes from his room upstairs on to the landing. He is wearing a much better tweed suit. He speaks as he opens his door

Victor Who's that down there? My God, Aubrey! (*He comes downstairs, speaking as he does so*) That's all right, Mrs Holley; thank you.
Mrs Holley I was jest about to go, sir, unless there's anything else.
Victor Nothing I know of. Only don't say I said so.
Mrs Holley (*with an amiable smile for Victor*) Not me, sir. I know better than that.

Mrs Holley goes off to the kitchen with the cleaner

Aubrey (*as Mrs Holley goes*) Bye-bye, Pussy.
Victor Will you stop behaving like that?
Aubrey Like what? (*He rises*)
Victor And I told you not to come here, didn't I?
Aubrey Not when she's in, you said.
Victor How were you to know?
Aubrey Know what?
Victor That she wasn't in, of course.
Aubrey Well, is she?
Victor No, thank goodness.
Aubrey Then what are you bellyaching about?
Victor I told you always to find out first.
Aubrey (*pitiably*) But I have found out, haven't I?

Aubrey's tone softens Victor, whose affection for Aubrey is never far from the surface

Victor All right, all right, my dear boy. But you know what it is.
Aubrey What what is?
Victor I'm being careful not to put her out. She's been considerate and cheerful; in fact quite gay at times, especially since her step-mother died. So long as she doesn't see *you* everything's fine. I'm absolutely in clover.

Aubrey Well, I'm bloody well not. (*He sits*)

Victor Now steady with that language. And don't be ungrateful, either. I've spent a lot of my own money in helping you along. I got you a decent room to live in. I found you a good job.

Aubrey I've chucked that.

Victor What? Aubrey, you haven't got the sack again?

Aubrey No, I tell you; I chucked it. It was a lousy job, Dad—buggering about trying to sell cars.

Victor (*losing patience*) My God, Aubrey, I don't know how I stick you. You are the biggest chump I ever . . . So what are you doing now? Nothing, as usual.

Aubrey I *am* doing something.

Victor You are? What?

Aubrey I'm an extra.

Victor An extra what?

Aubrey At that film studios. It's a damn good job. I get a quid for every day I'm there.

Victor And how often is that?

Aubrey (*gloomily*) Not frightfully often.

Aubrey's depressed tone softens Victor again

Victor Oh, my dear boy, I'm sorry I spoke like that. (*He pats his shoulder*) I know you do your best. I think about you a great deal, you know. Anyhow, you've got your room. I've paid your rent on that a month ahead.

Aubrey I know. I wish you hadn't, Daddy.

Victor (*heartily*) No, that's all right. I'm glad to.

Aubrey No, but I've quit.

Victor (*reacting again*) You've what?

Aubrey (*rising*) I've got another room pretty nearly as cheap.

Victor Where?

Aubrey The room you got was a lousy one anyhow, and the bloke who kept it is a frightful shit.

Victor But he was paid in adv . . . (*He gives up*) Oh, well, where are you now?

Aubrey Just along there. In Eaton Place. (*He jerks his thumb*)

Victor (*incredulously*) Eaton Place?

Aubrey It's a top room, a sort of attic. I think it's really meant for a skivvy but it's quite all right. It's got a basin and all that.

Victor But Eaton Place? How did you come to go there?

Aubrey That's really what I came to see you about. A girl found it for me.

Victor (*alerted*) A girl?

Aubrey She's got a flat on the floor below me.

Victor What girl? What's all this? Haven't I told you to be careful about women?

Aubrey You speak for yourself, old feller me lad.

Victor That'll do. Now—what have you been up to?

Aubrey Nothing. You can see for yourself. She said she wanted to meet you so I brought her along.

Victor What? Where is she?

Aubrey Outside. She was waiting while I had a look-see. I'll call her in. (*He opens the front door*)

Victor is anxious but curious

Victor Well, we mustn't be too long . . .

Aubrey (*calling*) Hi—come in—it's okay.

Victor Still I'd better find out about this.

Ella comes to the front door

Aubrey (*as Ella appears and passes him*) She isn't in. Only the old man.

Ella comes down to Victor. Aubrey closes the front door. Ella is an attractive and sexy girl of twenty-one. She is of provincial middle-class but bright and confident. She wears a neat and becoming but inexpensive summer dress and hat. Aubrey announces her from the doorway as she enters

Here she is, Papa.

Victor (*surprised by Ella's appearance*) Oh. How-do-you-do? (*He shakes hands with Ella*)

Ella How do you do, Mr Keene. My name's Ella—Ella Reed.

Victor Well, well. You mean to tell me you're a friend of Aubrey's?

Ella (*with a little laugh*) Yes. Why not?

Victor I'm very glad to hear it. Fancy poor old Aubrey getting off with a girl like you.

Ella (*seriously defensive*) It depends what you mean by getting off.

Victor Oh, no, no, no. I expressed myself badly.

Ella We're just friends, that's all. And I'm very glad we are. Aubrey's different from the others.

Victor I can well believe that. But where did you meet each other?

Ella At a Lyons tea-shop, actually. It was full-up and we shared a table and got talking.

Victor H'm. That was a bit forward, wasn't it? On somebody's part?

Ella Mine. I suppose I'm rather a forward girl. (*She smiles briefly*)

Victor begins to smile back but checks himself

Aubrey Well, come on, Pop.

Victor What d'you mean, come on?

Aubrey What you're always telling me—manners. Ask her to sit down.

Victor Yes, but you'd better not be here for too long. Very well; just for a minute . . . (*He indicates a chair*)

Ella Thank you. (*She seats herself*)

Victor (*sitting*) So you met and talked at Lyons. (*To Aubrey*) You must have got to know her very quickly.

Aubrey (*patting Victor on the shoulder*) I'll bet you would have too. (*He laughs, then sits*)

Victor What did you talk about?

Ella Oh, jobs and things. I'm by way of being an actress; or wanting to be.

Victor Are you, though? Have you been in anything lately?

Ella I've never been in anything at all. I get an odd day's crowd-work at Elstree or somewhere.

Victor Ah—on the films—an extra. So that's how Aubrey got on to that.

Ella Yes, I gave his name to my agent. But he's only done it about once. Poor Aubrey simply can't manage to get there early enough.

Victor (*beginning to get definitely hostile*) If you'll tell me something that poor Aubrey *can* manage . . .

Aubrey It isn't me we're talking about. (*He rises*)

Victor Yes, it is. (*To Ella*) He was in a perfectly good job . . .

Aubrey It was a lousy job . . .

Victor (*still to Ella*) You've taken him to a new room too, I hear. In Eaton Place. As if he could afford to live in this part of the world.

Ella Well, I couldn't, either. But I know the man who owns the house.

Victor Oh, so that's it?

Ella No, it's not. There's nothing like that about it. (*With a quick smile*) Not with him, anyhow.

This brings a sharp glance from Victor. Ella goes on resignedly

And I'm being turned out of the flat, in any case.

Victor Oh, and why's that?

Ella It's just the old story, Mr Keene.

Victor What old story?

Aubrey Wake up, Dad. She's broke.

Ella (*reprovingly*) Aubrey . . .

Aubrey Well, he's got to be told sometime. And he's not very quick off the mark.

Victor Ah, now we have it. (*To Aubrey*) So that's why you brought her here?

Aubrey Yes.

Victor Have you been taking money off Aubrey?

Ella No—well—we sort of help each other out when we can.

Victor (*rounding on Aubrey*) That twenty pounds I gave you the other day for a new suit and shoes and things? Where's the new suit? Where is it? That isn't it.

The front door opens. Victor turns with an alarmed exclamation

Oh, good Lord. (*He rises*)

Alma enters, carrying a shopping bag of the period. She wears a dress of good quality but of quiet taste and a hat. She shuts the door

Alma There. I'm back in good time.

Victor Yes, dear; better than I . . .

Alma (*seeing Aubrey*) What's he doing here?

Victor He brought this girl.
Alma Oh? Who's she?

Ella rises. She does not appear in awe of Alma

Ella Good morning, Mrs Keene. My name's Ella. I'm a friend of Aubrey's.

Aubrey moves slowly towards the front door whenever Alma is not looking

Alma Really? I'm surprised to hear he's got one.
Ella Aubrey wanted me to meet his father. Actually, we were just going.
Alma You looked to me to be sitting pretty squat. (*Controlling herself*)
No. But why did you want to meet my husband?
Victor All right, dear. I'll tell you when they've gone.
Alma But I'd like to know now.
Victor Well, you can guess—any friend of Aubrey's. They came to try
and get some money.
Alma I see. (*To Ella*) And what's Aubrey to you, may I ask?
Ella (*boldly*) Someone to be with, that's all. (*She goes and takes Aubrey's
hand*) I'm fond of Aubrey. I look on him as a sort of pet.
Alma Well, that's honest enough, but you must have very unwholesome
tastes.
Ella I don't think so. Besides, he's such a pleasant change.
Alma What from? (*She puts her shopping bag on the table below the sofa*)
Ella Oh, never mind. Come on, Aubrey, we'll go.
Victor No, wait a minute. (*To Ella*) I'm afraid this has got to be put a
stop to.
Ella (*challenging*) What has?
Victor I'm sorry, but I don't think you're the right friend for Aubrey.
Ella That's exactly what I am. And he for me.
Aubrey (*laughing*) I believe poor old Popsy thinks you're a tart.
Victor Aubrey—will you?
Alma (*genuinely puzzled*) A tart? What does he mean, a tart?
Victor It's a common term, dear—for a prostitute.
Alma (*in a shocked tone*) Victor . . .
Victor Well, you asked.
Alma (*to Ella*) And is that what you are?
Ella (*mildly*) No, I don't think so. No, of course not. I mean, I don't
get paid for it, or walk out on the streets or anything like that.
Alma Then what *do* you do?
Victor Yes, well, never mind, dear. She told me she was trying to be an
actress.
Ella That was the idea six months ago when I first came to London.
Alma Where from?
Ella Gloucestershire. My father's a house agent. My mother died and he
married again. To a woman I hate. I had a terrible row with my father
and left home. I wanted to go on the London stage because I'm good
at acting. I played the lead in all the local amateur shows. (*To Alma*)
You know—*Paddy-the-next-best-thing.* (*Dramatically*) All-of-a-sudden-
Peggy.

Alma (*recoiling*) Good gracious. (*She sits on the sofa*)

Ella But I never realized how hopeless it would be. (*She sits in the arm-chair*)

Alma And so now you've come here trying to get help?

Ella Oh, if only you'd let me tell you all about myself—but I suppose I'd only shock you.

Alma You've done that already. Because so far as I can understand you are telling me that you allow men to seduce you.

Ella Yes, well . . .

Alma It's a very distasteful subject and one which I know very little about . . .

Aubrey *I'll* bet. (*He sits*)

Victor (*in a savage aside to Aubrey*) You keep your mouth shut.

Alma But is that true?

Ella Yes. Well, no. Not seduce me exactly, because . . .

Alma Because what?

Ella Well, I don't object, you see. Well, to be perfectly honest with you, I enjoy it like everybody else. So long as it's with somebody I like.

Victor Alma, I don't want you to listen to this.

Alma (*snubbing him flat; with a trace of the flare-up*) Do be quiet. Go on.

Victor is so squashed by Alma that he lets this go. Ella is anxious to be allowed to tell her story

Ella It all began when I had a terrible disappointment. I got spotted in the film-crowd by a very well-known actor. He sent for me to see him in his dressing-room on the set.

Victor Who was he?

Ella I don't know that I ought to tell you.

Aubrey It was Fred Castle.

Ella Aubrey.

Victor (*impressed*) Fred Castle, good Lord. (*To Alma*) Even you have heard of Fred Castle.

Alma (*indignantly*) What do you mean, "even I"? I've seen him several times. George never missed one of those farces he's always doing. He's supposed to be very attractive to women. (*To Ella*) So you went to his room, did you? What did he say?

Ella (*with a little laugh*) I remember his first words. I'd better not tell you what *they* were.

Alma You'll tell me what I ask you. What did this Castle man say to you?

Ella He just sat and pointed at me and said, "You look to have a very good pair of charlies".

Alma (*again puzzled*) Charlies? What did he mean?

Aubrey Tits.

Alma Charlies? Tits? What are you talking about?

Victor Tits, dear; short for teats—or rather the same thing. (*Illustrating with cupped hands*) You know . . .

Alma Don't be so disgusting, Victor.

Victor (*roused*) Don't go on at me—it's not *me*. (*To Ella*) Keep it clean, can't you?

Alma (*to Victor*) Don't keep interrupting. (*To Ella*) What did you do then? Walked out, I should hope.

Ella Walked out? On Fred Castle? Oh, Mrs Keene, how could I? I thought my career was made. Naturally I did what he wanted.

Alma But do you mean to say *you* wanted to too?

Ella Of course. Well, I mean—Fred Castle—who wouldn't want to? Wouldn't you?

Victor Don't you speak to my wife like that. *She*, of all people.

Alma That'll do, Victor. (*To Ella*) What happened then?

Ella He took me out that night to Eaton Place to a house run by a man called Mr Morris.

Victor And what goes on there? (*Quickly and guardedly*) No, steady—I mean if it's anything too near the knuckle . . .

Ella Oh, it's nothing improper.

Aubrey (*confidentially to Victor*) Gambling, Papa.

Victor (*in a sudden shock*) What?

Ella Chemmy and roulette and things.

Victor can only glare

Mr Fred Castle doesn't really care for gambling. He's never been there since.

Victor But you have?

Ella Mr Morris asked me to come—back to entertain his men friends; and he rented me this little flat next door.

Alma To entertain the men friends there as well?

Ella (*nearly losing control*) Yes.

Alma And you tell me you enjoy doing that?

Ella Well, I can pick the men friends I like, can't I? (*Turning impulsively*) Come on, Aubrey; it's no good; we'd better go. (*She rises*)

Alma We haven't yet heard why you came here trying to get money.

Ella (*sitting*) Well, I owe Mr Morris for the flat. He wants it all by tomorrow morning or he'll turn me out.

Alma And how much do you owe him?

Ella And I've had to get food and stockings and everything.

Alma How much, I asked?

Aubrey I'll tell you. (*Rising*) She wants a hundred and seventy quid.

Victor A hundred and seventy—it's past belief.

Alma (*rising*) I'm afraid you're a very weak and immoral girl.

Ella (*gently*) I don't think I'm *weak*.

Alma (*beginning to get worked up*) There's no denying that you're immoral, is there?

Ella (*rising*) No, not if you're old-fashioned, I suppose.

Alma These men you take to your flat—don't they give you money?

Ella (*shrugging*) They mostly seem to think I do it for pleasure.

Alma And that's exactly what you do, or so you say. Why can't you take yourself in hand and resist?

Ella Mrs Keene, why should anybody try to resist a thing like that?

Alma (*still angrier*) But you *can* resist if you put your mind to it. You can fight against anything and overcome it. You can change your whole nature.

Victor By gad, that's very true, dear.

Alma (*at the flying-up stage*) I didn't ask you to comment.

Victor No, but if anybody's got a right to say that, it's you. You've proved it yourself. You've been wonderful.

Alma (*in a complete outburst*) How dare you talk like that in front of people? My goodness, Victor, it's incredible sometimes how stupid you can be.

Aubrey (*delightedly*) Wow.

Alma Take that creature away out of my sight and keep him there. Go on, go away, go out and take him with you. (*She picks up Victor's hat and opens the front door*)

Victor Now steady, Alma ...

Alma Go on, do what you're told. Go away, both of you. Go on. Go for a walk. And only *you* come back.

Victor I don't want to go for a walk. Now, Alma ... (*He attempts his "laughing at her" stunt, laughing falsely himself and pointing a fore-finger*)

Alma Stop that nonsense and it isn't what *you* want. (*To Aubrey*) Go on. You too.

Victor (*looking out of the door*) I think it's going to rain.

Alma Then take your umbrella. (*She throws an umbrella at Victor*)

Victor You'll be sorry for this, you know. Come along, Aubrey.

Victor takes his hat and umbrella and goes out

Aubrey follows Victor to the front door

Aubrey (*to Ella*) I'll see you later.

Alma You will not. I'll see to that.

Aubrey I wasn't talking to you, Honeybum.

Aubrey goes out

Alma closes the door, then goes through a little spasm of remorse, shaking her shoulders as though to shake the anger from her. She speaks as if to herself

Alma Oh, why do I have to get like that—I haven't been like it for so long. (*To Ella*) It's that ghastly Aubrey. Why did he have to bring you here?

Ella I'm sorry you dislike Aubrey so much.

Alma Dislike him—he makes me positively shudder.

Ella (*sharply*) You don't think I go to bed with Aubrey, do you?

Alma Oh, don't be so revolting and disgusting and shameless.

Ella Aubrey's just ...

Alma (*cutting in*) Never mind Aubrey. These other men. Apparently you
go with them right and left. And like it.

Ella But, Mrs Keene, doesn't everybody like it?

Alma (*emphatically*) No.

Ella But surely they ought to?

Alma (*with challenge*) Ought to?

Ella Well, if Nature tells you . . .

Alma Nature can be a savage and brutal thing. Look at tigers.

Ella I'm not talking about tigers.

Alma I am. And some men too, for that matter.

Ella But it isn't only that Nature urges you on to do it. It's so gorgeous
when you do do it. I don't see how it can be wrong.

Alma I'm not talking about rights and wrongs. It's this finding pleasure in
it. (*She sits in the armchair*)

Ella Well, if you don't, Mrs Keene, I'm very sorry for you. And for myself too. Because I've got in this awful mess and I was hoping for sym-
pathy.

Alma (*severely*) Don't you tell me that I'm unsympathetic.

Ella No, but I took it for granted that you still went in for it like everybody else.

Alma That'll do, thank you. (*She rises*)

Ella There are heaps of other girls like me, you know.

Alma I do not know and don't want to.

Ella I think most unmarried girls will soon be doing it as a matter of
course, like men do.

Alma I keep telling you I am not interested. (*She sits on the sofa*)

Ella (*sincerely baffled*) Honestly, you're awfully different from everybody
else about it. (*Sitting on the sofa*) I mean, for instance, look at my grandmother.

Alma Why should I look at your grandmother?

Ella She had a boy-friend in Bordighera, an Italian boy, a gigolo. She
used to spend every winter out there with him in Bordighera. Right up
to the time she was seventy.

Alma (*incredulously*) Seventy?

Ella Over seventy.

Alma Poor thing. She must have had a particularly nauseating type of
aberration.

Ella *I* don't think she was a poor thing at all. I think she got the best out
of life. I only hope *I* live to be seventy.

*Victor enters at the front door. He has regained his self-confidence and
his manner is rather bossy. He closes the door and speaks while hanging up
his hat and disposing of his umbrella*

Victor Aubrey made off somewhere so I've come back.

Alma Is it raining?

Victor No, but I'm not going to hang about out there. Besides, I want a
word with this girl.

Ella (*hopefully*) Oh, Mr Keene, do you? (*She rises*)

Victor Yes. About Aubrey. I'll find him somewhere to go. In fact, I've had a very good idea about that. But please understand I won't have you going about together.

Ella (*with spirit*) But you don't understand—I'm good for Aubrey. I stop him from doing silly things.

Victor Such as chucking his job and becoming an extra and getting mixed up with a gambling hell.

Ella (*turning to Alma*) Oh, Mrs Keene, do please make him understand. I've got to get this money right away.

Alma It's no good your looking at me like that. This is entirely my husband's concern.

Victor (*decisively*) Come along, now; I think you'd better go. (*He moves up and opens the front door*)

Ella goes up to the daor

Ella (*in the doorway*) Yes, very well. But what a pity. Because I'm sure you're both such kind people really.

Ella goes out

Victor closes the door and comes down

Victor There goes a minx if ever there was one.

Alma (*effusively penitent*) Oh, Victor, I flew up at you. I'm so sorry. I won't ever do it again.

Victor Oh, well. It may have been my fault.

Alma What do you mean "may have been"? Of course it was your fault.

Victor You can make amends, anyhow. I've got to find Aubrey somewhere else to live.

Alma (*sharply*) You're not going to bring him near *me*.

Victor No, listen; I've had a brainwave. I had it while I was waiting out there. Mrs Tucker.

Alma Mrs Tuck—you mean Lolly?

Victor Yes; that cousin of yours. When she called here that day she said she still had that house at Ealing and took lodgers. She might take Aubrey.

Alma Not if she knew him beforehand.

Victor (*moving to the desk*) She might. And in a nice healthy domestic atmosphere like that he might reform. He's very weak-minded. Try her, do. (*He picks up the telephone directory*)

Alma It wouldn't be fair on her.

Victor (*hastily*) She could find out for herself. Please, Alma. For my sake. You said you were sorry for flying up. Look up her number.

Alma accepts the book

Oh, thank you, dear.

Alma I won't have Aubrey coming in here to meet her,

Victor (*picking up the shopping bag*) Well—we'll see. I'll just take this through to the kitchen. I must get him away from that girl. Mustn't I?

Alma (*with a deep breath*) I never knew such girls existed. And there are numbers of others like her she says. What are we coming to?

Victor Oh, I dunno. This younger generation—all unsettled and restless.

Alma slowly turns the pages of the telephone directory as they speak

Alma These young women going to bed with men and—whatever the word is for it. What *is* the usual word for it?

Victor What? Oh, I—don't think we want to go into that.

Alma (*on a sharper note*) Why not?

Victor The er—the polite term for it is sexual intercourse.

Alma Oh, rubbish. And as if there could be a polite term for that.

Victor escapes with the shopping bag into the kitchen

Alma flips the pages more quickly to discover "Tucker" in the directory as—

the CURTAIN *falls*

SCENE 3

The same. Tea-time the same day

The tea-table is back in the same position as Scene 1, with three places laid, and a large tray with teapot, etc.

Alma, dressed as in the previous scene, is seated at the table on one side. Lolly is seated behind it. A third chair has been occupied and is now back against the wall. The cakestand remains alongside the table. Lolly, who is drinking tea, is a plump, jolly, outspoken woman of Alma's age. She is a good stage lower in the social scale than Alma, good-looking, well-dressed and evidently prosperous. Besides the tea-cup, she is holding a little napkin, with which she gives her mouth a quick wipe

Alma Would you like a piece of seed cake?

Lolly No, thank you.

Alma You didn't have much tea. I hope you had all you wanted?

Lolly Oh, more than enough, thank you. It was Victor who didn't. He was hardly here a minute.

Alma (*taking Lolly's cup*) He's looking for this—son of his. (*She collects the tea-things on the tray*) He's been trying to find him all the afternoon. Not that it matters. I wouldn't let you take him in, even for a night. That was Victor's idea. (*She rises and moves to the kitchen*)

Lolly Yes, well, I'll wait and see him, anyhow; just for Victor's sake.

Alma Would you mind opening the door?

Lolly Of course, dear. What am I thinking of?

Alma exits with the tray

Alma Thank you.

Lolly (*finding her lipstick and using it with a hand-mirror*) Anyway, it's nice to see you again and have a bit of a pow-wow. It was sad about your old step-mother popping off like that.

Alma enters with a crumb-brush and tray

Alma Was it?

Lolly Oh, well. I daresay it was one of those merciful releases. (*Producing a cigarette-case and lighter*) D'you smoke, Alma?

Alma No. I never have. Victor smokes his pipe sometimes. In his own room.

Lolly (*lighting up*) Ah, a pipe-smoker. Yes, I thought he looked that sort. Tweedy-suited kind of chap. Shall I sit here? (*She indicates the sofa*)

Alma Where you like.

Lolly (*sitting on the sofa*) He's nice, Alma. You make a good pick.

Alma He's been very kind to me, and considerate. (*With deeper feeling*) He's made me quite a different woman.

Alma takes the cloth from the table and folds it during the dialogue. She is in no hurry about it

Lolly Well, marriage can't have meant much to you before. Oh, not that I can talk. Fifteen years ago it is now since I bade farewell to Archie. Let's see—did you ever know Archie?

Alma (*coldly*) I saw him once; but I never had anything to do with him.

Lolly You must be about the only woman who didn't.

Alma puts the folded tea-cloth over her arm and picks up the cake-stand and crumb-brush

(*Continuing, in a sympathetic manner*) And your old George Millett—he was another of them, wasn't he?

Alma I don't quite know what you mean.

Lolly Well—another like Archie.

Alma But did you know George?

Lolly Yes, of course. Didn't you know I did? (*She quickly adds*) Oh, I didn't know him as well as he wanted me to. Don't think that.

Alma He was never very particular.

Alma goes into the kitchen

Lolly (*talking on during this*) Mind you, I'm not saying anything against your old George. He was a dear old boy. I don't blame you for sticking to him despite it all. But I *was* a bit surprised when you told me you'd gone and taken another one on.

Alma returns

Alma I wanted companionship. A man's companionship. I hate women. (*She resets the desk chair*)

Lolly (*readily*) Oh, so do I, dear. And this has turned out really well?

Alma (*with reserve*) Perfectly, thank you. George did everything he liked. Victor does everything I like.

Lolly Aren't you lucky? Oh, well; it's never too late.

Alma (*as if just for something to say*) I wonder *you* never married again. (*She sits*)

Lolly After what I'd been through with Archie? No, thank you. I've done better than that.

Alma How do you mean?

Lolly Archie was all right to begin with—as a lover and all that. That was his trouble, women. Like it is with all of 'em. Goodness knows he got all he could want from me.

Alma (*fighting shy of the subject*) You needn't go into any details.

Lolly (*oblivious*) Oh, I don't mind your knowing. He was one of those chaps that just have to have variety. Quite soon after we were married, off he went, fornicating all over the shop.

Alma Lolly, you're spilling ash on the carpet. (*She rises*)

Lolly Oh, sorry, dear. Even at home he was at it. I had to sack two of the parlour-maids. He even had a crack at the cook.

Alma There's an ashtray here somewhere. (*She takes an ashtray from the window table to Lolly*) There. (*She sits*)

Lolly Oh, thank you. So after I'd divorced Archie I said to myself, "Oh, all right, my lad. I'll take a leaf out of your book. I've got this house, plenty of rooms and no-one in them. I'll take lodgers—nice, attractive gentlemen bachelor ones." (*Laughing*) And that's what I've been doing ever since. I've got three there now. Life's one long razzle.

Alma has listened to this with growing resentment and incredulity. She exclaims almost involuntarily

Alma You too? You do that?

Lolly (*taken aback*) Well, of course. Why not?

Alma (*incredulously*) You keep men in the house and go to bed with them in turns?

Lolly Well, you needn't put it quite like that. It makes it sound a bit insincere.

Alma (*more and more worked up*) Insincere? I think it's horrifying.

Lolly Oh, come off it, Alma. You ought to be the first to sympathize. Your marriage was much the same as mine—sitting there alone at home listening to the wireless while your husband was off on his own, chasing every woman in sight. Why shouldn't I make up for lost time and enjoy myself?

Alma That's what I can't understand—your enjoying it.

Lolly (*catching some of Alma's vehemence*) But—God Almighty—haven't you always enjoyed it and don't you still?

Alma Very well, I'll tell you. I never let George touch me. He was quite willing not to. As for Victor, I told him from the start—no. And he doesn't mind either.

Lolly But why? What put you off it? Were you raped as a kid or something?

Alma Yes. On the first night of my first marriage: when I knew nothing about anything.

Lolly (*genuinely enlightened*) Oh-h, yes. I remember hearing now. Well, of course—if you get a shock like that when you lose your virginity . . .

Alma Didn't you?

Lolly Shock? (*Laughing*) I went into absolute transports. I remember how I made Archie laugh. I will say for him, with all his faults, he was a marvellous hand at it.

Alma Transports! It's beyond me. I met another one today who's—like you about it. And she's still only a girl.

Lolly (*quietly and kindly*) Darling, you're the only one I've ever heard of who's like *you* are.

Alma I shrink from the very thought of it; from the whole revolting messy awkwardness of what you have to do. I think the whole thing's disgusting and nauseating and that Nature or Providence or whoever is responsible ought to be thoroughly ashamed of themselves. They might at least have thought of something nicer *looking* for it to be done with. I can't think of anything more repulsive than the sight of a man with nothing on. All that hideous bundle.

Lolly (*honestly sympathetic*) Oh, you poor darling.

Alma You needn't pity me. I'm only too glad to have avoided all that side of life.

Lolly Life—you don't know what life means. You poor dear, you were scared and horrified at the start and went and cut yourself off from the loveliest thing in the whole of existence.

Lolly's kindly manner and words have their effect on Alma. She softens a little

Alma I know I'm different but I'd rather you didn't tell me any more.

Lolly It's my duty to tell you and your duty to listen. Your duty to yourself. To say nothing of your duty to Victor.

This really makes Alma sit up and take thought. There is a note of uncertainty in her reply

Alma Victor's quite contented. He never thinks of that sort of thing.

Lolly Oh, rats. All men do. Especially at his time of life; a man gets his second wind. Oh, dear. I hope he's not doing an Archie on you.

Alma A what?

Lolly Having a bit of his own on the Q.T.

Alma Don't you dare say such a thing about Victor.

Lolly No, of course not. Then all I can say is he's being very unselfish.

Alma Unselfish? Do you really imagine that?

Lolly I don't imagine it; I know it. It means more to a man that it does even to us; though for meself I don't see how that's possible. Oh, Alma dear; if only you'd let yourself find out what it's like to be a woman. To be clasped tight to a man with him absolutely part of you and with that lovely urge growing in you all the time—on and on, more and more, nearer and nearer until ooo—it happens and you hear a glorious burst

of bells and you're in Paradise—if ever Paradise could be such **Paradise**
as that.

Alma (*after a moment or two; half-heartedly*) I know most people do find it
attractive.

Lolly I can't bear to think of you missing it all your life. Try it while
you've still got plenty of time. And think what it would mean to Victor.

Pause

Victor enters at the front door

Victor No good. Not a sign of him. (*He hangs his hat up and comes
down*)

Alma Did you go to his room?

Victor Yes. The front door was open so I went right up there. Nobody
about at all.

Alma Well, it wouldn't have mattered in any case.

Lolly Oh, I'd have liked to have seen the boy.

Alma You wouldn't.

Lolly (*preparing to leave*) I'll be getting along now. (*Rising*) Thank you for
the nice tea, dear.

Alma Not at all. (*She picks up the ashtray and takes it to the kitchen door*)

Victor Must you go so soon?

Lolly Yes, I really must. My lodgers will be getting home. Good-bye,
Alma.

Alma Good-bye. (*Opening the kitchen door*) And—thank you for coming.

Alma exits to the kitchen

Victor escorts Lolly to the front door and lets her out

Victor Yes, it's been good to see you again.

Lolly Well, it's nice to do each other a bit of good when we can. Ta-ta.

Lolly exits

Victor closes the door and comes down

Alma enters from the kitchen

Victor What did she mean by that? I don't want any doing good to.

*From this point Alma's whole manner shows a marked change. She has come
to a decision and is amicable, eager and persuasive; with only an occasional
brief moment of impatience and irritation*

Alma Victor . . .

Victor Yes, dear?

Alma I want to speak to you.

Victor (*apprehensively*) Oh? Well—yes?

Alma I've been meaning to tell you. I saw you in a new light this morning.
I was very pleased with you.

Victor (*puzzled*) Why? When? What?

Alma The way you dealt with that girl. It showed how strong-minded you can be if you choose.

Victor Rather too much so, I'm afraid. Poor little fool. I didn't mean to be too aggressive.

Alma But I like you to be aggressive. I want you to be more aggressive.

Victor I've no reason to be, Alma.

Alma Yes, you have. Aggressive with me too. Especially with me. I've always been the one to lay down the law. You've been so gentle and—giving-in.

Victor No, no. I've tried to be helpful and—considerate.

Alma Yes, and I haven't.

Victor Oh, you have, Alma.

Alma I have not. You're my husband. The husband should be the one to dictate.

Victor I've had no reason to . . .

Alma Instead of which I've always been the one to dictate: "Do this; do that. I don't want you to do this. (*Meaningly*) I don't think we should do that."

Victor Well, but we've got along very happily. There's Aubrey, of course; but apart from him—I'm perfectly contented, Alma.

Alma Oh, I'm sure you're not.

Victor I am.

Alma No. In one way—in particular—I know I've been very remiss.

Victor (*suddenly enlightened*) Oh, that? Well, dear, that's been up to you. But perhaps now that your step-mother's dead and you've got all that much more, it may seem a trifle squinny.

Alma (*put out of her stride, annoyed*) What are you talking about?

Victor What *you* are. You mean my allowance.

Alma (*almost flying up with impatience*) I do not mean your allowance. I give you your whole board and keep and three pounds a week to say nothing of paying the whole of the rates and electricity and telephone . . .

Victor Yes, all right, all right . . .

Alma And *gas* . . .

Victor Yes, yes, all right. Now, Alma, don't begin . . .

A brief pause. Alma recovers herself, biting her lip

But if it isn't my allowance, what is it?

Another brief pause. Alma becomes gentle and almost pleading in her manner

Alma Victor . . .

Victor 'Mmm?

Alma Victor, I think I've been very behindhand in showing you affection.

Victor Oh, nonsense, dear; you've always been very affectionate.

Alma I mean affection in its deepest sense.

Victor Your affection has always been as deep as it can go.

Alma (*a flash of annoyance*) Oh, don't be dense. (*Recovering and becoming* *alluring again)* Deep. (*She moves close to him*) Deep. (*Her face close to his*) It.

Victor (*staggered*) It?

Alma It.

Victor (*incredulously*) Oh, not it?

Alma It. What Nature intended for a man and wife. Part of each other. In and in. Up and up. On and on. Nearer and nearer. Bells and Paradise.

Victor Good god. (*He sits on the sofa*) But, Alma, from the very start you said . . .

Alma (*sitting beside him*) I was prejudiced and—ignorant and dreadfully unfair to you. (*She kisses him suddenly*) Now! I am going upstairs to my bedroom. (*On the move*) You come, too.

Victor is utterly unprepared for this and very uncertain of his own desires and capabilities

Victor (*rising*) Now, hold on, Alma.

She halts and turns

This is something that Lolly has been gassing about.

Alma She made me realize—and she was quite right to.

Victor But I'd put all thoughts of that behind me.

Alma So had I. But now—oh, come along. I'm so inquisitive and stimulated.

Victor Yes, but I mean—in the middle of the afternoon and everything . . .

Alma (*hardening*) Don't you want to? Aren't you eager to?

Victor Yes, of course, if you are. But it's so unexpected.

Alma Doesn't that make it all the better for both of us?

Victor Yes, but it's a thing you have to . . .

Alma (*still more challenging*) Have to what?

Victor Well, sort of—have to think yourself into.

Alma Why? Because I'm undesirable and off-putting?

Victor No, no, no; of course not; it isn't only that . . .

Alma Then what is it? Have you been doing an Archie on me?

Victor A what?

Alma Going with other women behind my back?

Victor Alma—how can you speak like that?

Alma Then why aren't you running upstairs after me? *Bounding* upstairs?

Victor I am. Only give us a chance.

Alma (*seizing his lapels and shaking him*) Then come on, will you?

Victor (*making the best of it*) Rather—you bet I will.

Alma changes again to glad excitement. She releases his lapels; puts her hands on his shoulders for a moment

Alma Oh, Victor . . . (*She goes quickly upstairs*)

Victor follows slowly. Alma turns half-way up the stairs

Come on, Victor!

the Curtain *falls*

ACT II

SCENE 1

The same. Shortly after ten that night

The lights are on and the curtains drawn, though it is still dusk outside

Victor, in a darker suit and tie, is sitting in an armchair reading the evening paper, and, for the first time in this room, smoking a pipe. There is a small table beside his chair.

Alma, in a stylish semi-evening dress, enters from the dining-room armed with a poured-out drink on a tray. She is in a very amiable mood. Victor's attitude at the opening is self-assured, and indeed rather patronizing

Alma Here, dear.
Victor (*glancing up*) Mm?
Alma A whisky and water for you. I thought you might like one tonight.
Victor Oh, thanks. Put it down there, will you?

Alma puts the tumbler on the little table. She stretches her limbs and then goes and reclines on the sofa. She smiles at her thoughts for a moment or two, then speaks

Alma Oooo—I feel so radiant, Victor. Wasn't this afternoon wonderful?
Victor (*looking up from the paper with a short smile*) I'm very glad you found it so.
Alma Well, you did too.
Victor (*with a brief chuckle*) M-hm.
Alma Oh, Victor; it can go on and on now, can't it? There's still a long time for us ahead.

He is reading again; she speaks rather more pointedly

Isn't there?

Victor takes a sip of the drink and replaces the tumbler

Victor Yes, dear, but . . .
Alma But what?
Victor It's not a thing you want to have a—well, a set time-table about.
Alma (*ignoring this*) After all these years, suddenly to discover—and you were so considerate.
Victor Oh. Thank you, dear. (*He gives another brief chuckle*)
Alma I mean it was so thoughtful of you to take so long about it. (*Brief pause; then, rhapsodically*) I got the bells. Did you get the bells?
Victor What bells?

Alma When it happens you seem to hear bells.

Victor Do you?

Alma Don't *you*?

Victor Well, I dunno—that sounds a bit high-falutin to me.

Alma Dear Victor, I know you were thinking only of me. I could tell that from what you said.

Victor (*apprehensively*) Why, what did I say?

Alma You said, "Thank God I brought it off".

He takes another sip, puts the tumbler back and rises

Oh, Victor, isn't it wonderful to know that we possess such a treat?

Victor (*putting the newspaper on the table*) My dear Alma, I'm very glad for you; especially now when you're getting on in life. But it's not a thing you want to overdo.

Alma I don't see how one could possibly overdo it.

Victor Oh, one can, you know.

Alma I can quite understand Lolly going on as she does. That girl this morning too—even at her age.

Victor What I mean is it's apt to take it out of you.

Alma Oh, yes; but only for that lovely minute with the bells.

Victor Yes, but quite apart from these bells . . .

Alma (*with a note of anxiety*) But, Victor; you do love it. Don't say you don't.

Victor I don't. I mean I don't say I don't. I do. Love it I mean.

Alma (*stretching out her arms to him*) Well, then . . .

The front-door bell rings. They are both very surprised

Who on earth can that be?

Victor I can't think. Somebody from outside wanting something.

Alma Someone come to the wrong house. You'd better see.

Victor (*going to the front door and calling*) Who is it? (*He opens the door*)

Aubrey appears. He is dressed just as before

Aubrey Oh, hallo, Pop.

Alma (*rising*) Send him away.

Victor (*to Aubrey*) What do you want?

Alma I won't have him in here.

Victor No, hold on, Alma. I've been trying to find him ever since this morning.

Alma It's my house, isn't it?

Victor Yes, but dash it he *is* my son.

Alma (*indignantly*) Very well, see him. So long as I don't. I'm going to my room.

Alma goes upstairs, but remains on the landing, listening. Victor admits Aubrey and shuts the front door

Victor (*bluntly*) Come in, then.

Aubrey comes down and picks up Victor's drink

Aubrey Hallo, what's this?
Victor (*following him down*) Leave that alone. That's my drink.
Aubrey Good for you. I'll bet you don't often get a piss-up.
Victor (*taking the tumbler from Aubrey and putting it back on the table*) What have you come for? And at this hour of night.
Aubrey I had to come. It's about Ella.
Victor That girl? No, thank you. I'm through with her.
Aubrey It's frightfully urgent. She's had an offer.
Victor Thank goodness for that.
Aubrey She's in a frightful mess, and wants your advice.
Victor She's had all the advice she'll get from me.
Aubrey Oh, don't be bloody about it, Dad. She's brought a bloke along.
Victor What? She's not here again, is she?
Aubrey Yes. Outside.
Victor Send her away.
Aubrey But this bloke's here, too.
Victor What bloke?
Aubrey A bloke named Felix. He comes from Morris's place.
Victor (*indignantly*) What are you talking about?
Aubrey He's Morris's stick-man.
Victor Stick-man?
Aubrey You know, the bloke who rakes in the doings. (*He imitates a croupier*)
Victor (*very incensed*) You mean you've brought some damned hanger-on from that gambling-den to this house?
Aubrey Ella got him to come along to show you she was on the level. (*He turns towards the front door*) I'll get 'em in.
Victor (*taking a step to prevent him*) No. I won't have it.
Alma (*from the landing*) Yes, she can come in.
Aubrey Oh, good egg! (*He opens the front door and calls*) Come right in.

Alma comes downstairs. Victor turns to her, protesting

Victor But, Alma . . .
Alma I want to see her again. She interests me more than she did.

Ella, entering, hears this last line and responds gladly

Ella Oh, thank you, Mrs Keene.

Ella is followed in by Felix and Aubrey. Felix comes right in. Alma speaks as Aubrey follows

Alma But not you. You can wait outside.
Victor (*to Aubrey*) You hear that? You wait out there.
Aubrey No, thanks.

Victor (*changing to sympathetic persuasion*) Go on, Aubrey, there's a good chap.
Aubrey (*disgustedly*) Oh, shit.

Aubrey exits

Victor closes the front door

Ella I'm awfully sorry to trouble you again, Mrs Keene, but something ghastly has cropped up.
Alma What is it now?

Ella presents Felix. Her manner towards him is aloof and unfriendly

Ella I've brought this man . . .
Alma I heard about him, thank you. What's he got to do with it?

Felix is about thirty-five. He is dark—he looks as if he were a Cypriot, but if so he has lived in England most of his life, for his English is perfect, in fact profuse, with a common and just very slight accent

Ella His name's Felix.
Felix Pleased to meet you, madam.
Ella I don't know whether he's got any other name.
Felix (*jokingly*) Oh, a large selection.

Alma sits on the sofa

Ella And this is *Mr* Keene. (*She indicates Victor*)
Felix Pleased to meet *you*, sir.
Victor (*glaring at him*) You won't be for long. You help to run this gambling-den?
Felix That is so, yes. I'm what you might call a junior partner. Like I understand you are here.
Victor If you're going to start by being insulting . . .
Alma (*quietly*) No, don't be aggressive, Victor.
Victor (*in a hurt tone*) Oh, it's *don't* be aggressive now.
Alma (*calming him*) Just until we've heard . . . (*To Ella*) Do you want to sit down, my dear?
Ella Oh, thank you. (*She sits beside Alma*) Shall I tell you what's happened?
Alma I'd like to do some talking first. (*To Felix*) You gave this girl a flat next to your building . . . ?
Felix Not me. I didn't. That was Mr Morris. It's him that owns the property.
Alma But why is she being turned out now without proper notice?
Felix There again, that's Mr Morris. But he considers she's had ample time to settle her losses and her back rent and that. He told her so six weeks ago.
Victor (*to Alma*) But there's something about an offer, dear. I don't know what it is.
Ella I can tell you that. Felix has offered me another flat to go to. (*Angrily, to Felix*) Go on—*you* tell them.

Felix I haven't offered—not me in person. It's just I have a friend who's willing to give her accommodation.

Victor (*scornfully*) A gentleman friend, no doubt?

Felix A perfect gentleman. He moves in the highest circles.

Alma (*optimistically*) Oh, well . . . (*To Ella*) Is he somebody you know and like?

Ella shakes her head: Alma is disappointed

Oh.

Victor (*challenging Felix*) What you mean is some man wants to keep her?

Ella No, it isn't that. If it was that I might . . . (*To Felix as before*) Tell them.

Felix (*to Victor*) It isn't he wants to keep her, sir; not in the sense you mean, speaking no doubt from your own vast experience.

Victor is about to protest violently; Felix beats him to it and continues

More like—maintain her. In a swankey way and at a very high-class address.

Ella (*with emphatic scorn*) Yes, Duke Street, St James's. They want me to become a whore.

Victor (*to Felix*) You unutterable swine.

Alma No, Victor . . .

Victor But damn it . . .

Felix (*politely*) Again, it is not me, sir. I don't mind what she does. I am the mere mouthpiece for my friend.

Alma (*amicably to Felix*) I expect you're really my friend himself.

Felix I only wish I was, madam. He's in very much better off circumstances than me. Or Mr Morris, either. No, my friend picked on her principally by reason of her being a girl of class. Oh, looks as well, granted; but class, that's what they go for my friend's clientele. They're very high-class themselves; guards officers and the like. Two or three M.P.s in their time off—Conservative ones, needless to say. Men of title even.

Victor Alma, I don't like you listening to this.

Alma Why on earth not? It's most interesting. Quite a revelation. (*To Felix*) Men of title, you say?

Felix (*warming to it*) Oh, yes, madam. (*Sitting*) In that quarter of the West End; all top-notchers.

Alma (*genuinely interested*) Goodness.

Felix (*encouraged; concentrating on Alma*) And then country gentlemen in town for the night and rich American visitors and so on. Oh, it's a very fruitful field.

Alma I'd no idea of all this. Really, it's quite fascinating.

Victor (*barely audible in protest*) Alma . . .

Felix And not only nights, of course. There's a very sizeable afternoon clientele.

Alma (*for her own benefit*) Afternoon—Oh, yes—I can quite believe that.

Felix Yes, there's quite a number of respectable old middle-aged customers show their preference for matinée performances.

Victor That's enough. Get out of this house!

Alma (*to Victor*) Oh, do stop interfering. This is something I've never heard about and I want to. (*To Felix*) And do you mean she'd simply live in this smart flat and sit there waiting to be called on?

Ella, who has been sitting bottling up her indignation, now butts in angrily

Ella (*rising*) That's what they like to make out. It doesn't mean that at all. It means walking the streets at night with the police after you, and goggling at every vile man you meet. Doesn't it? (*She prods Felix*)

Alma Does it? (*To Felix*) Would she have to do that?

Felix Yes—it would mean she would have to walk around . . .

Ella There—you see?

Felix But round there, up and down Jermyn Street, it's a very exclusive beat; so long as she steers clear of the cheaper sister'ood. Some of those foreign ones can be very nasty with their handbags.

Victor Now, that'll do. Alma, I simply won't . . .

Alma Wait a moment, Victor. (*To Felix*) Now, you.

Felix At your service, madam.

Alma Oh, not at mine too, I hope. But tell me this. If she did this, would she still have to pay what she owes at your gambling place?

Ella (*vehemently*) Yes. That's how they want me to raise the money—this filthy way.

Alma (*to Ella*) Oh. (*Rising*) I thought perhaps you *wanted* to do it?

Ella Wanted to? Would you want to? Having to give yourself to the first brute of a man who came along.

Alma (*still quite intrigued*) Oh, but you could always choose only nice-looking ones.

Ella That's just what you can't do. (*To Felix*) Can you?

Felix (*to Alma*) No, madam. (*Rising*) With all his good qualities my friend would hardly stand for that. Outside of her own clientele she'd have to accommodate whatever comes along.

Ella (*to Alma, anxiously*) There you are! You see? After what you said this morning you must be horrified?

Alma Never mind what I said this morning. I was hasty and inconsiderate. There is that actual pleasure you spoke of.

Ella (*sitting*) Well, Mrs Keene, I don't want to be rude, but I just can't make you out.

Felix Of course, she'll have to face up to some formidable unpleasantness . . .

Victor That's enough from you.

Alma sits

(*Moving to the front door*) You get out.

Felix (*to Ella*) Well, there it is—Mr Morris says he's got to have the money tomorrow morning. (*To Victor*) That's okay. I have no desire to outstay my heart welcome.

Victor (*opening the front door*) I ought to inform the police about you. You'll be lucky if I don't.

Felix No, sir. I think you will be the lucky one.

Felix goes out

Victor shuts the door on him quickly and comes down, speaking as he does so

Victor God, what skunks there are in the world. (*He quickly finishes his drink, clamps the tumbler on the table and rounds on Ella*) How dare you bring a man like that into my wife's house?

Ella I had to bring him; to make you believe the trouble I'm in.

Victor You're in no trouble whatever, or needn't be. You can easily get a respectable job . . .

Ella Well, you've seen for yourself what may happen to me if you don't give me the money.

Alma All of these other men you've been so friendly with—won't one of them . . .?

Ella (*cutting in*) I don't know where they are. Or even who they are.

Alma Ask your grandmother—the one that goes to . . .

Ella Bodrighera?

Alma Bordighera.

Ella (*sarcastically*) I can't very well do that; she's dead.

Alma (*thoughtfully*) Oh, yes; I suppose she very likely is.

Victor (*in an aloof, rather sneering tone*) Why not the fellow who started you off? The man who first *took* you to this ghastly gambling place?

Ella (*startled*) Who?

Victor Your friend Fred Castle.

Alma Of course. Victor, how clever of you.

The suggestion has flabbergasted Ella. She does her best to hide this

Ella Oh, but, no, really—I couldn't possibly do that.

Alma Of course you can. And taking you to the place wasn't all he did to you, was it?

Ella I don't think he liked me much. He never did anything else for me. I think I disappointed him.

Alma (*rising*) Well, if you won't tell him I'll tell him myself.

Ella (*rising*) Oh, Mrs Keene, you mustn't.

Victor No, steady, Alma.

Alma (*rounding on Victor*) Why? It was you who suggested him. Where is he acting now?

Victor At the Leicester Theatre, I suppose. He always is.

Alma Well, he'll be there now. If we go at once we can catch him.

Victor What? No, Alma, hold on. We can't do this.

Alma Well, if she won't go by herself we'll go with her.

Ella, who has been taking thought, now chimes in readily

Ella No, all right; I'll go. After all, he can't kill me.

Alma No, you kill him. Be firm with him. You don't know how to treat men. Except, I suppose, in bed.

Victor Alma, Alma . . .

Alma Don't keep on "Alma, Alma", and wasting time. (*To Ella*) Go at once and catch him. You'd better take a taxi. (*To Victor*) Give her the money for a taxi.

Victor resignedly searches in his pocket

Victor Probably get there quicker by tube. Still . . .

Ella I'll do my best with Mr Castle but if he won't help me, Mrs Keene, can I come and see you again?

Alma (*sitting on the sofa*) Not tonight.

Victor No, we've done what we can. You've had your chance. Here's for your taxi. (*He gives her some money*)

Ella (*quietly*) Thank you.

Victor opens the front door

Alma Now go along quickly.

Aubrey appears in the doorway. Ella passes him and goes

Aubrey Cuckoo.

Victor You go away too. Go on.

Ella (*from outside*) Come along, Aubrey.

Aubrey Gosh. D'you mean he's coughed up?

Aubrey disappears quickly

Victor shuts the door

Alma Bolt the door.

Victor You bet I will. (*He bolts the door*) I've had enough of that young woman. As for her bringing that swine of a fellow . . .

Alma Yes, but it was interesting to hear about prostitution. What a pity there's such a disagreeable side to it.

Victor (*sitting beside Alma*) Alma—honestly, I don't know what's come over you. It's that Lolly. Ever since she came you've been a different woman.

Alma (*at her gentlest*) Yes, bless her for it. Oh, Victor; I wish I'd known about it all along.

Victor Oh, well. Better late than never, or whatever the saying is. (*He pats her hand and turns away. He wants to get off the subject*) I wonder whether that girl will find a taxi. (*He rises*)

Alma (*changing to the practical*) Why? You mean she won't be in time to catch Fred Castle?

Victor (*unconcernedly*) Oh, I should think so.

Alma He ought to be told to wait and see her. (*She rises*)

Victor (*rather more anxiously*) No, no; he'll still be there.

Alma (*moving to the desk*) I think I'll just make sure. (*She sits and picks up the directory*)

Victor (*alarmed*) No, Alma; steady. What are you up to? (*As she begins to search the pages*) No, Alma; think what you're doing. We don't want to get involved in this.

Alma (*as she turns the pages*) Well, it was you who sent her to him.

Victor But there's no need for him to know that. Do be careful, Alma.

Alma Leicester Theatre, Stage Door. (*During the next lines she dials, moving her eyes to and from the book*)

Victor Wait, will you. Listen, Alma. We can't get mixed up——

Alma (*cutting in*)—Will you stop interfering.

Victor No. You told me to assert myself and I'm damn well going to.

He tries to get at the receiver. She pushes him back. He half stumbles and by the time he has recovered himself she has dialled and is listening

It may lead to some hideous row.

Alma (*with a violent gesture at him*) Quiet, will you? (*On the telephone*) Are you there? . . . Yes. I want to speak to Mr Castle, please. . . . Still what? . . . On stage? You mean he's still acting?

Victor Thank God for that.

Alma (*on the telephone*) Well, give him a message, please.

Victor No.

Alma (*flapping at Victor and continuing*) He's to wait there, please, until a young lady gets there to see him. . . . No, I can't remember her name but it's important he should see her because she's in trouble and it's really Mr Castle who's responsible.

Victor (*horrified*) Alma. Oh, my God.

Alma (*with another quick flap at Victor*) What do you say? . . . Never mind all that; just . . . Certainly, it's Mrs Keene. . . . Yes; twenty-nine A Brompton Mews. Keene, with an "e" on the end. Keene . . . K—double e—n—e. Keene. . . . (*Sharply*) I beg your pardon?

Victor (*in a last desperate effort*) Here, give me that. Let me speak to him.

Alma (*not yielding the receiver*) Are you there? . . . (*To Victor*) It's no use; he's rung off.

Victor I'm not surprised.

Alma He seemed a very ill-mannered man.

Victor Do you realize what you told him to tell Castle? That the girl's in trouble and he's responsible?

Alma Well, so he is. (*She rises*)

Victor But, Alma, that can only mean that he's put her in the family way.

Alma Oh, rubbish. And what does it matter, anyhow? The girl will soon tell him if it isn't that.

Victor (*relieved*) Oh yes, that's true. But he'll want to know what *you're* up to.

Alma She can tell him that too. (*She goes to the window table and pours a drink*) I'm a friend who's trying to help her.

Victor (*half-heartedly*) Well, let's hope so. (*He sits*)

Alma Of course. (*With a benign smile*) Stupid.

Victor But listen, Alma. This is the end of it about this girl. I'll get Aubrey away from her somehow and then that's done, finish.

Alma (*giving Victor the drink*) I suppose she'll have to go to Duke Street.

Victor She'll get there sooner or later—you said so yourself. (*Accepting the* *drink*) Thank you, dear. I'm sorry for her in a way but I'm not going to have you upset. (*Thinking aloud*) We've had enough for one day.

Alma (*affectionately*) Dear Victor—you don't call *today* upsetting, do you? (*She sits*)

Victor (*responding*) Oh that. I'm delighted about that. Anything to make you happy. (*In a practical tone, with a glance at his watch*) Come on, dear; it's time we went to bed.

Alma Oh, rather! (*She rises*)

Victor After all that I'm feeling pretty fagged out. (*He rises*)

Alma Oh, I'm not. I'm feeling quite gay. You go and get into your pyjamas and then come along to my room.

Victor What?

Alma Well, what do you suppose?

Victor Oh, but, Alma dear, don't . . .

Alma Don't what?

Victor Don't—don't please have any ideas about now—again.

Alma (*in a hurt, not angry, tone*) You mean you don't want to?

Victor Tonight? Alma, it isn't possible. I mean a man of my age, it absolutely whacks him. For quite a time.

Alma (*rather mischievously*) Listen. I had a lovely hot bath this afternoon—you know, afterwards. It made me feel so wonderful, so exhilarated. Why don't you go and have a bath?

Victor (*firmly*) I fully intend to have a bath, but not with any idea of exhilaration. I mean to have a good long soak.

Alma Well, do. Soak as long as you like and then come and tell me how you feel.

Victor I'm sorry, Alma. Definitely not tonight.

Alma Oh, Victor.

She looks suddenly fiery and he anticipates her volubly

Victor It's just that you've had this experience now suddenly late in life or rather, in middle-age or whatever it is, and you've found it very agreeable and exciting and all that and you want to go right ahead and carry on with it all the time—I believe women can do that much more than men, I don't know. But men can't—at any rate *I* can't. I never could.

Alma (*still fiery*) After all this time—and I came round to it—chiefly for your sake because of what Lolly said about your being unselfish about it—and now I find how wonderful it is and what I've been missing—(*pointedly*)—and *you too* . . .

Victor (*aggressively*) That's no reason to turn it into a sort of smash and grab thing. (*More appealingly*) It's meant for people who feel deeply for each other at the right time.

Alma Right time? When? When next?

Victor Alma, it isn't a thing you can have a regular set schedule for. (*Compromising*) Well, I don't know—I believe the working classes do sort of earmark Saturday nights . . .

Alma What? Only once a week?

He shrugs

I must be very mistaken in my idea of the working classes.

Victor I mean—people at our time of life. I think once a week is supposed to be—about it.

Alma makes no reply. She turns and sits on the sofa with a quick, impulsive sitting action. Victor deliberates for a moment and decides not to continue the argument

Well, I'm going up now. (*He goes to the stairs*) Are you going to bed, dear?

Alma (*dully*) Not yet. You go to your bath. I'll do the lights.

Victor Oh, right you are. (*Turning on the stairs*) Goodnight, dear.

Alma does not reply

Victor goes upstairs and into his room

Alma remains on the sofa as though deliberating a desperate problem. Her lips move to her thoughts and she is scarcely heard murmuring the words "Once a week". Her body makes a slight swaying movement as she sits. Then comes a sudden sweeping change. She gets as intense a "flying-up" fit as ever before. She rises, picks up a cushion, flings it to the floor. Then she kicks it, and strides upstairs, as—

the CURTAIN *falls*

SCENE 2

The same. About 11.30 the next morning

Mrs Holley is standing in the middle of the room looking at a shopping bag. She calls up towards Alma's bedroom

Mrs Holley Madam! I'm going . . . I say I'm going, madam! Huh. None so deaf as them that doesn't want to.

Mrs Holley exits to the kitchen. Victor enters from his bedroom, with binoculars. He calls to Alma's closed door

Victor Well, I'll be off to Lord's, dear.

Mrs Holley enters

Good morning, Mrs Holley. (*He comes downstairs*)

Mrs Holley Good morning, Mr Keene.

Victor Why, what's up, Mrs Holley? Why have you got your hat on?

Mrs Holley I'm off.

Victor Anything wrong?

Mrs Holley Yes, sir, not that there's often anything right. But this morning . . .

Victor Why, what's happened?

Mrs Holley Madam, comes in here with her shopping; starts in on me—why hasn't this bin done, why hasn't that. Go on, then, she says, take this stuff into the kitchen, talking to me as if I was some sort of Native.

Victor Yes, well, listen, Mrs Holley. Don't take it to heart. Between you and me, she's rather upset about something that went wrong.

Mrs Holley What went wrong, sir?

Victor I've no idea.

Mrs Holley I done nothing to upset her.

Victor No, no, she was like it before you got here. Now please, Mrs Holley, do all you can to make her, you know, like she generally is.

Mrs Holley Like she generally is who to?

Victor Please, Mrs Holley. for me. (*He hugs her*)

Mrs Holley Just for you, sir.

Victor Tha-at's better.

Mrs Holley Thank you, sir.

Mrs Holley exits to the kitchen with the basket. Alma enters from her bedroom with a travel brochure

Alma What were you saying to Mrs Holley?

Victor Oh, nothing, dear. She was just messing about in here. I'm going to Lord's now. Is that all right?

Alma (*coming downstairs*) Why shouldn't it be all right?

Victor Yes, well, have a nice day, dear. (*Pausing as he goes up*) Alma . . .

Alma Yes, what?

Victor Alma, is anything the matter?

Alma The matter? What do you mean?

Victor Only you seem rather, well, distant to me this morning.

Alma Do I?

Victor Mrs Holley seemed a bit put out. Did you have a row with her?

Alma One doesn't have rows with servants. I had occasion to speak to her.

Victor When I came down she was leaving.

Alma If she wants to leave she can. (*Calling into the kitchen*) Mrs Holley . . .

Mrs Holley (*off*) Yes, madam.

Alma You can go if you wish.

Mrs Holley Oh, thank you, madam.

Victor Just for the day that is.

Alma Well, of course for the day. What do you suppose?

Mrs Holley enters and moves towards the front door

Mrs Holley Good day, madam. Good day, sir.

The front doorbell rings. Mrs Holley opens the door

Ella is standing there

Ella Is Mrs Keene in?
Mrs Holley She is if you want her.

Mrs Holley exits

Ella Thank you. Oh, Mrs Keene.
Alma Yes. Come in. Shut the door, Victor.

Victor closes the door

Ella I hope you don't mind my coming here again.
Alma No, I want to hear what happened with that Castle man. (*She sits*)
Victor Did you see him?
Ella Yes, of course.
Victor What did he say about my wife?
Ella About who?
Victor About my wife. What did he say?
Ella Nothing. Why should he? He doesn't know you does he?
Alma Never mind about me. What did he say about you?
Ella Oh, need you ask. (*She sits*) He said what I knew he would. He said
    I was a fool to get mixed up with Morris and it was nothing more to do
    with him.
Alma So what are you going to do now?
Ella What can I do?
Victor I told you that yesterday. Go and get yourself a respectable job.
Ella Oh, Mrs Keene, please make him understand. I've got to get this
    money right away.
Victor No you haven't. Just clear out and leave. Morris can't do a thing.
Ella Oh, very well then, you've got to be told the whole truth.
Victor I've been told all I want to hear.
Alma No you haven't.
Victor What? Why not?
Alma Because I haven't. Go on.

A car is heard to drive up outside and sound its horn

Ella You're not going to like this.
Victor Oh, that'll be a nice change.
Alma (*interrupting*) Wait a moment. What's that car doing there?
Victor Car?
Alma (*pointing at the window*) There. Outside.
Victor It can't be coming here.
Alma Then why has it stopped outside my house?
Victor Half a tick—I'll see. (*He steps to the window and lifts a corner of the
    lace curtain. He looks out then reacts violently*) Good God; it's Fred
    Castle.
Ella (*in sudden panic*) Oh, no. (*She rises*)
Alma (*in a satisfied tone*) Then he did get my message.

Ella Your message?
Alma (*rising*) About you. Last night. I telephoned him.
Ella But I didn't see him. I lied to you. Oh, don't let him know I'm here.

The doorbell rings

I'll tell you everything when he's gone. I was just going to. Oh, please don't tell him. I'll wait in here.

Ella scoots into the dining-room. The dining-room door remains a crack open

Victor (*in a dither*) Oh, good Lord, Alma . . .
Alma (*calmly*) Let him in, can't you?

Victor opens the door, revealing Fred Castle. He is about forty—very trim and well-turned-out. He is autocratic, completely the boss and not to be argued with; but with a sense of humour and a candour which are entirely sympathetic. He is at first in a very challenging mood

Fred Is there a Mrs Keene living here?
Victor Yes. I'm her husband.
Fred *Are* you though?
Victor Please come in.
Fred You bet I'll come in.

Fred walks in. Victor closes the door

Alma I am Mrs Keene.
Fred Really. My name is Fred Castle.
Victor (*gushing*) Yes, yes. You need no introduction.
Fred (*to Alma*) Was it you sent me that telephone message last night?
Alma Certainly it was. Why?

Fred looks slightly puzzled but is still on the offensive. He turns and looks at Victor

Fred That's an M.C.C. tie you've got there.
Victor That's right, yes. I'm a member.
Fred Oh. I didn't know they admitted blackmailers.
Victor (*more alarmed than affronted*) What? Really, Mr Castle—blackmail—that's a very ugly word.
Fred Ah. I see you know the right dialogue, too. Yes, it *is* an ugly word. (*Looking at Alma*) And it applies to some very ugly people.
Victor My wife didn't mean what she said on the phone.
Alma Victor, how dare you say that? Of course I meant it.
Victor Oh, do shut up.
Alma (*angrily*) What?
Victor (*to Fred*) I heard what she said about your getting a girl into trouble. Of course to you that can only mean one thing.
Fred Oh, thank yer.

Victor She didn't mean it that way at all.

Fred Then why didn't you stop her saying it?

Victor (*with desperation*) Have you ever tried to stop a telephoning woman?

Alma (*sitting on the sofa*) I'll tell you what I meant, Mr Castle. You took a girl to a gambling place kept by a man named Morris.

Fred Did I? When? And why shouldn't I, I'd like to know?

Alma Did you or did you not?

Fred Don't you question me. I've come to do that to you. You said this girl was coming to see me last night.

Victor Yes, but now she says she didn't.

Fred I know she didn't—why not?

Victor There's something very fishy about this.

Fred (*indignant*) I'll say there is. Why d'you think I've come here?

Victor (*passing Fred to get to the dining-room door*) Excuse me.

Fred *Excuse* you—that's a good one. Come on, what *is* this little game?

Victor (*opening the dining-room door*) Come out here.

Ella comes in

Ella and Fred face each other in silence for a moment; Fred with a frown as if searching his memory

Ella I don't suppose you remember me?

Fred Eh? Oh, yes. I do. It wasn't so long ago.

Alma You saw her in a film studio and told her she had a nice pair of charlies.

Victor (*alarmed*) No, Alma—really.

Alma Well, that's what began it; according to her.

Fred Yes, I daresay I did. And I don't think I was far wrong.

Alma Then you took her to this Morris's and then took her home and had social intercourse.

Fred (*with a glance at the despairing Victor*) I'm glad I was so refined about it. (*Indignantly again*) And what the devil has that got to do with you? Are you her parents or something?

Ella No, they're only trying to be kind. Only I'm desperately wanting some money and they thought I'd better ask you first. Only I didn't dare.

Fred No, but it seems you get around telling people about me.

Ella No, only them. It's not a thing I boast about. Because I'm afraid I must have been rather a flop.

Fred (*more amicably*) You needn't think that. I like to mix it, you know. I don't go in for permanent attachments.

Alma That's true of all the men who have made reputations as great lovers.

Victor Alma, be careful what you're saying. You can't talk to Mr Castle like that.

Alma But it's a compliment. Everyone knows that Mr Castle is very attractive to women. Aren't you?

Fred Well, that's my good fortune, isn't it? (*Guardedly*) In some cases.

(*Breaking off, to Ella*) What's all this, this trouble you're in? What happened to you?

Ella That night Mr Morris asked me to come back. So I did. Then he sort of took me up and rented me a flat next door, to entertain his men friends. So I did that too. But not for money. And I got awfully into debt.

Alma So now she's being turned out of the flat.

Fred (*not over-concerned*) Oh, dear.

Alma But she has got an offer to go to Duke Street and become a tart.

Victor Prostitute, dear.

Alma Oh, don't be so pernickety. (*Fred sits*)

Ella I only told you that as a sort of last effort to get the money. I got Felix to come along and help.

Victor You're the most unscrupulous girl I've ever heard of.

Ella Yes, I expect I am. (*She sits*) Because, if you must know, I don't need the money for the flat. I paid Mr Morris a week ago.

Victor and Alma are open-mouthed

Victor ⎱ Paid him? How could you? ⎱ (*Speaking together*)
Alma ⎰ Paid him with what? ⎰

Ella is silent for a moment; then speaks as though against her will

Ella Aubrey got the money for me.

Victor (*incredulously*) Aubrey?

Ella From the car place he had a job at.

Victor You mean to say they let him have it?

Ella No. Some customer paid a hundred and forty pounds for a car in cash. And Aubrey kept it.

Victor Stole it?

Ella Yes.

Victor Oh, my God.

Fred Who's Aubrey?

Alma His abominable son. Not mine, thank you.

Victor He's simple-minded.

Fred He sounds pretty capable to me.

Ella His boss was away at the time. He came back two days ago. I knew he'd find out so I went and talked to him.

Victor Walker?

Ella Yes. He was very angry of course. But I got him to give me till today to pay him back. But he's going to run Aubrey in if the money isn't paid this morning.

Victor But, good heavens, it's nearly twelve now. (*In a great flap*) Hold on—I'll phone Walker. No, that's no good; he calls himself the something motor depot. The what motor depot? Oh, damn it, I've forgotten. Do you remember?

Ella I'm afraid not. I wrote it down but I haven't got it here.

Victor Why not? Oh, hell.

Fred (*rising and taking Victor aside, confidentially*) Steady, now. You seem to be in what is commonly known as a bugger's muddle. You know where this motor place is, anyhow?

Victor Yes, very close here, thank God. End of Brompton Road by the *Oratory*. I'll go there at once.

Alma (*who has been regarding Victor's flap rather disdainfully*) Take your cheque-book.

Victor Yes, yes; I have it on me; but . . . (*He pulls up, faced by a snag*)

Alma (*with quiet command*) Pay the man.

Victor (*effusively*) May I do that? Oh, thank you, Alma.

Alma Then don't waste any time.

Victor No fear. I'll run all the way.

Fred You can take my car if you like.

Victor Oh, thank you, but it's no distance.

Fred It'll save you getting apoplexy. Come on; I'll tell my feller.

Fred goes to the front door. Victor hurries after him

Victor (*as he goes*) This is immensely kind of you. .

Fred Oh, that's nothing.

Fred and Victor disappear leaving the door ajar

Ella turns to Alma. Ella does not appear very penitent

Ella (*rising*) Oh, Mrs Keene, I hardly know what to say.

Alma You don't often have that trouble, do you? Tell me this, did you ask Aubrey to steal it for you?

Ella Well, it was sort of—between us . . .

Alma All these lies—that other nonsense about Duke Street . . .

Ella (*with greater assertion*) No, that was true. I did get that offer. It still holds good.

A car is heard starting up and driving away

Alma Then that's where you'll finish, I should think. Wretched girl. (*She turns aside angrily*)

Ella tries a bit of blarney

Ella Oh, Mrs Keene, if ever it looks as if I might really have to go to Duke Street, do you think I could come and see you again then?

Alma turns as if to rend her. She glares at Ella and speaks angrily

Alma Yes.

Fred enters through the open doorway and comes down

Ella (*to Alma*) Shall I wait until Mr Keene comes back?

Alma No, certainly not. (*She rises*)

Ella Then I'll go now. Thank you, Mrs Keene. Good-bye. Good-bye, Mr Castle.

Fred (*airily*) Oh, good-bye, my dear. Glad to have seen you again.

Ella (*without any sarcasm; rather artificially coy*) Oh, I'm so glad you're glad. Good-bye.

Ella goes

Alma (*as Ella goes*) Go on: go on and close the front door, please.

Fred closes the front door

Thank you for lending my husband your car. It was very thoughtful.

Fred Well, he seemed a bit het up. I don't mind waiting a few minutes. This is all a rather unusual experience for me.

Alma It certainly is for me—to have a little while alone here with you of all people. (*Pointedly*) With your reputation.

Fred (*quite sincerely*) I just happen to be what I am. One thing, thank goodness—I don't need flattery. I never flatter *myself*. In fact, it gets rather a bore at times being so much better than anyone else.

Alma Oh, I didn't mean your reputation as an actor.

Fred (*with instinctive resentment*) Why, what more d'you want? (*Quickly urbane again*) Ohh, you mean the horses? (*Surprised*) Why, are you a race-goer?

Alma No, no, Mr Castle; I mean what I said before—your reputation as a ladies' man.

Fred (*laughing*) Oh, so that's it? Well, I'm not supposed to have many rivals in that field either. (*Leg-pulling*) So that's where your tastes lie, is it?

Alma (*dead seriously*) Yes. That's why it's so helpful to be able to consult an expert. You see, I've only just become interested in the physical side of it.

Fred Why, have you been in a nunnery or something?

Alma Yes. For over twenty-five years. In a nunnery of my own making.

Fred Pity you left it so late to come out.

Alma (*sitting on the sofa*) Not too late. But I don't suppose a man like you would want to be bothered with my case; odd though it is.

Fred I like oddities. I didn't know there were any left.

Alma Please don't laugh at me. I know I'm middle-aged and undesirable.

Fred I didn't mean it that way.

Alma Yes, you did. It serves me right for talking to you like this.

Alma is genuinely upset with herself. Fred sees this and becomes gentle and sympathetic

Fred Now, now—don't upset yourself. (*Confidentially*) I'll tell you something. I've had pretty nearly every desirable young woman who's available and quite a few who aren't. I don't say I get tired of them, but just now and then, there's something about a middle-ager—well, say forty-odd—which offers a new sort of kick.

Alma A beautiful woman though . . .

Fred Doesn't follow. As a rule the lovelier a woman looks the dumber she comes. It's personality that counts.

Alma Oh, Mr Castle. I think it's wonderful of you to be so versatile. Do you think I've got personality?

Fred You bet you have.

Alma (*brightening*) You mean I might possibly be one of these middle-agers who could offer a new sort of kick?

Fred (*slightly compromising*) Well, let's say—I didn't think there was much novelty left. But if there is you're certainly a starter.

Alma You're really laughing at me the whole time, aren't you?

Fred Not at all. I'm always ready to encourage an enthusiast.

Alma Then you're just being kind to me.

Fred Well, why not? Come on—snap out of all this droopy stuff. It's a thing to be bright about and—sporty.

Alma Oh, Mr Castle. You're making me feel more optimistic every moment.

Fred I'll tell you something else. (*Sitting beside her*) Women who are past the early stages have got another consolation.

Alma Oh, what?

Fred (*putting his arm round her*) They're always the most passionate.

Alma Oh, Mr Castle, are they?

Fred Always.

Alma Oh, Mr Castle; you've got your hand on my charlie.

Fred It's just making itself at home. (*Removing his hand and sitting up*) But I don't quite get this—have you been married long?

Alma A few months.

Fred Is that all? It seems a bit soon for you to be on the general rampage like this. Isn't he up to the job?

Alma (*rather incoherently*) No. Oh, yes. At the time it was wonderful and I got the bells and he brought it off thank God and everything. But he's no good about wanting and enthusiasm and oftenness enough.

Fred A bit past it, eh? Poor devil. I hope I never get that way. You must have a heart, you know. Don't tick him off about it. If you want to bring him up to scratch do it gently and fondly—you know—a little monkey business.

Alma Monkey business? Oh, Mr Castle; what do monkeys do?

Fred (*laughing to himself*) Oh, good Lord, we're back in the kindergarten. Here—turn your face here. (*Taking her face he brings it to his*) Open your mouth a little.

Alma opens her mouth

No, just a little crack.

A silent scene follows in which he plays on her lips with his tongue. She opens her mouth and he inserts his tongue. Alma works herself up into a passionate state. She grips his hand and takes it to her breast. At length, with an effort, he frees himself and laughs

There you are. That's what's generally referred to as the guzzle. Does it give you ideas?

Alma (*wildly exclaiming*) Ideas. (*She seizes him*)

Fred Steady now.

Alma Guzzle me again. Guzzle me.

They kiss

Fred (*getting himself disengaged*) My word. You're that novelty all right.

A car horn is heard. The shadow reappears on the window. Fred turns his head towards it

But you'd better return to normal. (*Rising*) Your old man's back.

Alma Bolt the door.

Fred No, thank you.

Alma Oh, how exasperating.

Fred Your hair's a bit wonky.

Alma I don't care. (*Nevertheless she tidies it as she goes on*) Well, at least I can say I've been guzzled by Fred Castle. (*She rises and goes to the mirror*)

Fred (*with assumed severity*) Now, don't *you* start.

Victor enters hurriedly, leaving the door open

Victor It's all right—it's settled. He was pretty nasty about it but he took my cheque. (*To Fred*) I'm very grateful to you, Mr Castle.

Fred That's okay. I've got to get along now.

Victor Thank you for waiting. I'm sure it's been a great treat to my wife.

Fred For me too. (*He gives Victor a mischievous dig*) You don't realize how lucky you are.

Victor Oh, I do indeed.

Fred (*to Alma*) You keep him up to that. Good-bye.

Alma (*almost inaudibly*) Good-bye.

Fred turns to the door

Victor I'm sorry I've been such a bad host. I ought to have offered you something.

Fred Your wife did that.

Fred goes

Victor follows into the porch and gives him a wave of the hand. Then closes the door and turns, as the car is heard going and the shadow disappears

Victor My word, what an awfully nice chap.

Alma How much did Aubrey steal?

Victor A hundred and forty pounds.

Alma I'll tell the bank to pay it to your account.

Victor Oh, thank you, dear Alma. Doing this for my sake—it's wonderful.

Alma So long as you guarantee that I never see Aubrey again. (*She sits on the sofa*)

Victor Absolutely. What a business all round. To think that Fred Castle would ever come to this house. I must say he was awfully agreeable and helpful, wasn't he?

Alma (*flatly*) Very.

Victor How did you get along with him?

Alma We just chatted. He was very pleasant. Aren't you going to your cricket?

Alma is only half-listening; she is trying to decide whether to tell him something

Righto then. (*Picking up his binoculars*) I'll be off. (*Getting up*) Good-bye, dear, and thank you again for what you did.

Alma (*as he gets to the door*) No, Victor. (*Rising*) Wait a moment.

Victor (*turning back*) Yes, what?

Alma You were quite right about me this morning. I was in a very bad mood. It was because of last night—your not wanting to—go on.

Victor Well, never mind that now. That's all . . . (*He breaks off with a gesture*)

Alma Let's be honest about it. You don't really ever want to do that, do you?

Victor Well, Alma, we were very happy together before it—cropped up.

Alma But don't you really ever have any sort of—(*making an urging gesture*) feelings that way?

Victor Well, I'm a normal man, of course. One occasionally—thinks about it.

Alma Haven't there been any times since we married when you wanted?

Victor Oh, yes, I suppose—mildly.

Alma But you've never done it? I mean with anybody else?

Victor Of course not.

Alma Why of course? I would have, if I'd been you.

Victor (*nettled*) I don't mind telling you I nearly did once.

Alma (*keenly enthusiastic*) Oh Victor, when?

Victor I was on top of a bus. It came over me unexpectedly, like a sort of itch. It happens that way. Especially on the tops of buses.

Alma Poor Victor. But you resisted?

Victor Oh, it passed off. I forgot it when I got to Lord's. I saw Duleep make a hundred.

Alma You're quite right about how we were getting to be happy together. I don't want to upset that. So I've decided something. I'm going away.

Victor (*in great surprise*) Away? Where?

Alma I don't know where. Just for three or four weeks perhaps.

Victor But why on earth—what's the id . . .? (*With sudden challenge*) Alma—what's the idea?

Alma (*decisive and practical*) Mrs Holley will see to you—I'll arrange all that. And I'll give you quite enough to keep you going.

Victor What's behind all this? I can't help suspecting something and I don't at all like it.

Alma I can't help that. I've got to do something about myself.

Victor Now listen, Alma. If this is what I think I won't stand for it.

Alma Are you the one to say? (*Brief pause*) Go on—go to your cricket. (*She sits on the sofa*)

Victor again turns towards the front door; pauses in thought. He takes a step down towards Alma and speaks gently

Victor Alma, just sit and think it over quietly. Don't go and ruin our whole life together. You don't seem to realize how fond I am of you.

Alma rises

Alma (*flying up*) Do you suppose I'm not fond of *you*?

Victor gives up. He takes his hat and walks out, closing the front door

Alma deliberates for a moment, then goes to the desk with the travel brochure. She picks up the telephone, sits, finds a number in the brochure, and dials

Alma (*after listening for a moment*) Are you there? . . . Is that Messrs Thomas Cook and Sons?

the CURTAIN *falls*

SCENE 3

The same. Ten o'clock at night, three weeks later

All the lights are on, and the curtains are drawn

Victor, wearing a dressing-gown and pyjamas, is standing by the window table drinking a glass of brandy. He pours another glass. A taxi is heard approaching. Victor looks out of the window, then finishes his drink hurriedly, moves down to a table and empties the ashtray into a wastepaper basket. He replaces the ashtray, then takes the drinks tray into the dining-room. The taxi door slams. Victor hastens to the stairs, switches off the lights, then runs upstairs, switches off the landing lights, and goes into his bedroom

Alma enters from the front door carrying a coat and vanity case. She switches on the lights by the front door, then puts the case by the window. A Taxi-driver enters with a hatbox and suitcase

Alma Just put them down there, please.

He puts the cases by the window. She pays him

Thank you.

The Taxi-driver inspects what she has given him, gives a slight jerk of the head, and goes

Alma shuts the front door and draws the bolts

Victor enters on to the landing and switches on the landing light

Victor Alma—good Lord—you've come back home again. (*He starts down the stairs*)

Alma That's fairly obvious, isn't it? Well, Victor?

Victor Good Lord, this is beyond anything.

Alma What is?

Victor Your suddenly turning up after all this time.

Alma It's only three weeks and a bit.

Victor Yes, but I'd have come and met you. If only you'd have let me know you were coming.

Alma It's just as well I didn't. I'm about three hours late. Something went wrong with the cross-Channel boat. They had to go and get another.

Victor Poor Alma, you must be fagged out.

Alma No, not in the least. I just sat and waited.

Victor Have you had any dinner?

Alma Oh, yes; a very good one. They saw to all that.

Victor Oh, good. But will you want something else before you turn in? A cup of tea or anything?

Alma (*casually removing her hat and coat and laying them aside as they talk*) No, thank you. And I'm not going to turn in just yet.

Victor Well, I'd better take your things upstairs, anyhow.

Alma No, leave them alone for now. I want to sit and hear all about you.

Victor Me? Oh, I've got along all right—as best I could.

Alma You've been looked after properly? Has Mrs Holley been behaving herself?

Victor Oh, fine. I've been going out for my evening meals. I did tonight. Then I came back and was reading in bed and heard you arrive.

Alma And Aubrey? What have you done about him?

Victor Nothing. That girl's still looking after him. I've just let it rip. I don't know what else to do.

Alma (*sitting on the sofa*) Well, now about *my*self—I've decided to tell you everything. I want to tell you all that happened to me straight away. I feel I should sleep better.

Victor (*sardonically*) I wonder if I will.

Alma No, I'm afraid you won't.

Victor For heaven's sake, let's keep it till tomorrow.

Alma No. Now sit down, Victor.

Victor (*greatly against his will*) Oh, all right then. (*He sits on the armchair*) Let's have it.

Alma You can smoke your pipe if you like.

Victor No, no; I've finished with all that for the night. I've cleaned my teeth and everything.

Alma Then just listen and don't keep fidgeting. Well, you know what my motive was in going abroad, to Bordighera.

Victor Yes, but—go on.

She glances at him sternly

Alma I didn't like it at first.

Victor Why only at first?

She gives a quiver of impatience at him. He makes a gesture of apology

No. All right. Carry on.

Alma There weren't many people in the hotel. A few American married couples and one old permanent Englishman. It was hopeless for me there, hopeless. I thought I'd come on a wild goose chase. I got almost frantic . . .

Victor Oh, Alma, do you have to tell me all this?

Alma Yes. I want you to realize what happened to me, and to try to understand. Just to show you the sort of—turmoil—I was in; there was a valet in the hotel who did the shoes. A regular valet, quite a smart, well-mannered young man. I got him to bring my shoes into my room in the morning. On the second morning he brought them in, I came out of my bathroom by mistake on purpose with nothing on.

Victor (*staring and shaking his head*) It's beyond me. What happened then?

Alma He ran away, screaming.

Victor I expect he thought *he'd* surprised *you*, and was screaming in apology.

Alma Don't try to be kind, Victor. It made me despair of myself. Then suddenly, ten days ago, it came my way—the complete fulfilment I was looking for.

Victor (*rising quickly*) That's enough. I don't want to hear any more. A wife coming home and telling her husband——

Alma (*cutting in sharply*) —Well, you knew what I'd gone for. You must listen.

Victor I will not.

Alma You must.

Victor (*moving to the cases*) I'll take these things upstairs and go to my room. And you too. To yours.

Alma (*rising*) Not yet, Victor, until I've told you everything—I want you to take pity on me and help me to decide.

Victor (*with challenge*) Decide what?

Alma What's going to happen to me now. And to you. Please, Victor.

He gives in without saying anything. She goes on as before

I hired a car to have a drive round the country. The driver was a young Italian, very bronzed and handsome and speaking very good English. I asked him whether he was married and he said no, he had too many girl friends to want to get married. I told him he ought to try going with a plain, middle-aged woman because I'd heard from a friend of mine who was a great connoisseur, that they were the women who were the most exciting and passionate and gave kicks.

Victor Alma, this is incredible; it simply isn't you. What in God's name has happened to you?

Alma He took me for miles to an empty farmhouse he knew of. It was all locked up but there was a nice clean barn.

Victor A barn? (*He sits on the sofa*) Good God, Alma, this is the most degraded thing I ever heard of. Like a dirty French farce.

Alma (*sitting in the armchair*) I couldn't help that. I'd found what I'd

been longing for and it was more wonderful even than I'd hoped. I left
the hotel and rented a little furnished villa by the week. He came in his
car every afternoon. It was—(*closing her eyes*)—oh—beyond all words.
(*Opening her eyes*) The great thing was he appeared to be quite inex-
haustible.

Victor Thank you; it's bad enough without any sarcasm. I wonder how
much you had to pay this bastard.

Alma I gave him what he wanted—I didn't care. But that was really the
trouble; that's what led to it.

Victor Led to what?

Alma It was three days ago—it seems like weeks . . .

Victor What does?

Alma He came to the villa as usual, all gay and debonair and paying me
compliments. He started to undress me . . .

Victor You can spare me the details . . .

Alma Then he began whispering about how he'd got into money trouble,
and would have to sell his car and wanted me to give him a great deal
more and when I said no he began shouting and threatening me; I
thought he was going to kill me. And it was all so shaming because
besides being frightened I had nothing on above my waist. I was like
one of those Greek women from some vulgar piece of old statuary,
struggling with some heathen male creature who is trying to get at her
handbag.

Victor (*rising, forgetting himself in indignation*) The stinking Dago brute—
by gad, I wish I'd been there.

Alma Oh, Victor, I wish you had. He threw me on the bed and got my
bag and threw my traveller's cheques at me and took all my Italian
lire and dashed off in his car. So I went straight to the telephone—that
is, directly I'd got my camisole on again . . .

Victor And phoned the police . . .

Alma Police? No, of course not. I gave up the villa and booked to come
back here today. (*Brief pause*) So here we are. (*Sharply*) And don't go
on being angry with me; that won't do any good.

Victor Oh well—I don't suppose I've any right to be.

Alma Yes, you have. But please keep it to yourself. Because if you're
going to stay on with me after this . . .

Victor We'll thrash all that out tomorrow. (*Going up to the cases*) Now,
for goodness sake, go to bed. (*He takes up the two suitcases*) I'll take
these up.

Alma But, Victor, I want to get things settled about ourselves.

Victor Yes, but not tonight.

Alma You're ashamed of me, aren't you?

Victor No. What you do is up to you. It always has been. Don't forget
your coat and things. (*He goes to the bottom of the stairs*) Don't bother
about the lights; I'll see to them.

Alma (*picking up her coat and hat*) You needn't think I'm ashamed. Yes,
I am. But I'm only ashamed of being so vain as to think that any man
would really want me like that.

She starts upstairs, Victor following

I suppose my bed's made?

Victor (*on the landing*) Oh Lord, I hope so. Yes, I expect Mrs Holley will have seen to that.

Alma (*opening her bedroom door*) It looks to be all right.

Alma goes into the bedroom

Victor (*speaking into the room*) Well, there you are. (*He puts the cases inside*) Don't be too long getting to bed. Good night. (*He turns away*)

Alma comes out of the bedroom

Alma Leave the landing light on. I'm going to the bathroom.
Victor Oh, are you? Yes, of course. Right you are.

Alma goes into the bathroom and shuts the door

Victor starts downstairs and stops half-way, looking anxious

Lolly, fully dressed and carrying a hat and handbag, comes quickly, and in a very surreptitious manner, from Victor's bedroom

There is some dumbshow, Lolly wanting to escape and Victor signalling that Alma is only in the bathroom and for Lolly to go back to his room. Lolly, despite this, comes impetuously down, pushing past Victor and making for the front door. She unlocks this, but does not realize that it has been bolted. She then tries to unbolt it, but finds it difficult. Victor goes to her aid, getting Lolly out of the way and pulling back the bolt

Alma comes out of the bathroom, her toothbrush in her hand, and stands watching

Victor opens the front door

Lolly hurriedly escapes

Victor finishes bolting the door. He looks over his shoulder, and sees Alma. She comes downstairs slowly and calmly and does not speak until she is at the bottom and face to face with Victor

Alma Was that Lolly?
Victor Yes.
Alma Has this been happening often?
Victor No, this is only the second time. Soon after you went away Lolly rang up. I said you'd gone abroad for a little change. So she asked me to take her out to dinner. And—oh, well . . .
Alma Why did you say yes?
Victor Well, dash it, I was lonely. I wanted company and she was very

friendly and we had rather a lot to drink at dinner and there it was.

Alma And now again the second time.

Victor She invited herself again. I couldn't very well say no. You wouldn't want me to hurt her feelings.

Alma What about my feelings?

Victor (*boldly*) Well, think what you were doing.

Alma You didn't know what I was doing.

He makes a helpless gesture. She continues volubly

I've been completely open with you—poured out my troubles. You weren't going to tell me a word about yourself and Lolly.

Victor (*lamely*) The husband isn't supposed to.

Alma You're really just as bad as I am and even worse.

Victor You began it.

Alma Never mind who began it. Can't you see what this means? I come home to you and make a clean breast of all that happened to me, half expecting you to turn away in disgust and leave me. And now what do I find? That you're as bad as I am and even worse and we're back where we were before.

Victor (*hopefully*) Oh, Alma; can we be?

Alma It isn't can we be, it's what we're going to have to be. Of course it will be much easier for you than for me. You only did what you did out of silly weak-mindedness. You never think of that sort of thing as a rule. You said so yourself.

Victor Now and then, I said. (*Meekly*) Well, but we've still got affection. At least, I have.

Alma Haven't we both? Are you accusing me of not being affectionate?

Victor No, no. But that'll help, won't it? Because affection really counts for more than the other thing, doesn't it?

Alma I daresay it *does*. Yes, of course it does. Except at the actual time.

Victor Try to overcome this other thing, Lolly.

Alma (*fiercely*) What?

Victor I mean Alma. Try to overcome it.

Alma I'm going to. I've got to, haven't I—if there's nothing else for it?

Victor And if there's anything I can do . . .

Alma The only thing you can do is never never to let the subject be mentioned between us again.

Victor No. We'll be like we were before any of this ever happened.

Alma I've said so already, haven't I? (*Moving to the stairs*) Now—I'll go and start my unpacking. You go to bed. I'll bring you your tea in the morning as I always used to.

Victor (*relieved and pleased with himself*) Thank you, dear Alma.

Alma mounts two stairs and turns

Alma Just one thing.

Victor (*amiably*) What is it, dear?

Alma Don't ever let Lolly know that I know.

Victor Know what?

Alma Don't be stupid, Victor. Don't ever let Lolly know that I know what you did with her tonight.

Victor Of course not. As a matter of fact, I didn't. You came barging in before we'd even started.

Alma (*with slow, joyful surprise*) Ohhh—oh, then you're still . . .

She runs down at him, throwing her toothbrush in the air. He catches her in his arms

Oh, Victor—how splendid. Come along.

They both run upstairs, Victor leading Alma. As they disappear into his bedroom—

the CURTAIN *falls*

FURNITURE AND PROPERTY LIST

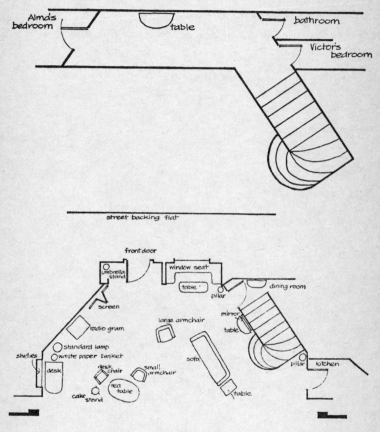

ACT I
SCENE 1

On stage: Sofa. *On it:* cushions
Large armchair
Small armchair
Desk chair
Desk. *On it:* telephone, telephone directory, blotter, small vase of
    flowers, dressing

Radiogram. *On top:* small vase of flowers
Wastepaper basket
Occasional table (*beside sofa*)
Occasional table (by stairs). *On it:* lamp, pot plant
Window table. *On it:* ashtray, magazines
Folding tea-table. *On it:* cloth, tray with milk jug, sugar bowl, 2 cups,
    2 saucers, 2 knives, 2 plates, 2 napkins
Cake-stand. *On it:* muffin-dish with scones
Screen
Umbrella stand. *In it:* Victor's umbrella
On hook by front door: Victor's hat
On window-seat: cushions
On wall below stairs: mirror
On front door: bolts

Off stage: Tray with teapot and hot-water jug **(Alma)**

SCENE 2

Strike: Tea-table
            Cake-stand
            Vase from radiogram
            Vase from desk

Set: Desk chair by desk
            Small armchair up C
            Cleaner and duster C

Off stage: Shopping bag **(Alma)**

SCENE 3

Strike: Victor's hat and umbrella

Set: Tea-table as Scene 1. *On it:* cloth, 3 cups, 3 saucers, 3 plates, 3 nap-
            kins—all used; large tray with teapot, milk jug, sugar bowl, hot-
            water jug
            Desk chair and armchairs round table
            Cake-stand with cake
            Telephone directory in original place
            Alma's handbag on small armchair

Off-stage: Crumb-brush and tray **(Alma)**

Personal: **Lolly:** handbag with lipstick, cigarette case, lighter, powder compact

ACT II

SCENE 1

Strike: Tea-table
            Alma's handbag

Set: Desk chair at desk
            Small armchair upstage

Large armchair down R
Small table below large armchair. *On it:* pipe, ashtray, matches,
    newspaper
Window curtains closed
On window-table: tray with drinks, whisky decanter, water jug, glasses
    —1 glass already poured

Personal: Victor: coins

SCENE 2

Strike: Drinks tray
              Ashtray
              Pipe
              Matches
              Glass

Set: Window curtains open
              Telephone directory on desk
              Clean ashtray on occasional table
              Shopping bag C

Off stage: Binoculars **(Victor)**
              Travel brochure **(Alma)**

SCENE 3

Strike: All flower vases
              Travel brochure
              Ashtray

Set: Window curtains closed
              Key on outside of front door
              Full ashtray on occasional table
              On window-table: tray with brandy decanter, soda syphon, 2 glasses—
                  1 already poured

Off stage: Vanity case **(Alma)**
              Suitcase, hatbox **(Taxi-driver)**
              Toothbrush **(Alma)**

LIGHTING PLOT

Property fittings required: table lamp, standard lamp, wall brackets, landing light:
   3 switches—by front door, kitchen door, and on landing
Interior. A living-room. The same scene throughout

ACT I, Scene 1.   Day
To open: Effect of April afternoon sunshine
No cues

ACT I, Scene 2.   Day
To open: Effect of August morning sunshine
No cues

ACT I, Scene 3.   Day
To open: Effect of August afternoon sunshine
No cues

ACT II, Scene 1.   Night
To open: All practicals except landing light on
No cues

ACT II, Scene 2.   Day
To open: Effect of bright August morning sunshine
No cues

ACT II, Scene 3.   Night
To open: All practicals on

Cue 1	**Victor** switches off room lights	(Page 51)
	Snap off all interior lighting except landing	
Cue 2	**Victor** switches off landing light	(Page 51)
	Snap off landing light	
Cue 3	**Alma** switches on room lights	(Page 51)
	Snap on all room lighting	
Cue 4	**Victor** switches on landing light	(Page 51)
	Snap on landing light	

EFFECTS PLOT

ACT I

SCENE 1

No cues

SCENE 2

Cue 1	After CURTAIN up *Doorbell rings*	(Page 12)

SCENE 3

No cues

ACT II

SCENE 1

Cue 2	**Alma:** "Well, then . . ." *Doorbell rings*	(Page 31)

SCENE 2

Cue 3	**Mrs Holley:** "Good day, sir." *Doorbell rings*	(Page 41)
Cue 4	**Alma:** "Go on." *Car drives up, horn sounds*	(Page 42)
Cue 5	**Ella:** "Oh, don't let him know I'm here." *Doorbell rings*	(Page 43)
Cue 6	**Ella:** "It still holds good." *Car starts up and drives away*	(Page 46)
Cue 7	**Fred:** "You're that novelty all right." *Car drives up, horn sounds*	(Page 49)
Cue 8	**Fred** goes *Car starts up and drives away*	(Page 49)

SCENE 3

Cue 9	**Victor** pours brandy *Taxi drives up and stops*	(Page 51)
Cue 10	**Victor** enters *Taxi departs*	(Page 51)

MADE AND PRINTED IN GREAT BRITAIN BY
LATIMER TREND & COMPANY LTD PLYMOUTH

MADE IN ENGLAND